T0271089

Foreign Aid in a World in Crisis

This book investigates the geopoliticisation of foreign aid in recent years, against a background of global overarching crises such as climate change, conflict, Covid-19, economic crisis, energy shortages and migration.

Foreign aid has historically been understood as assisting both with the development objectives of the recipients and with the trade and geopolitical interests of the donors. In the first decades of the 21st century, however, this balance has been shifted by a series of complex global challenges. This book argues that donors have now moved towards framing aid as a geopolitical instrument, wherein aid can be given or withheld based on power or political intent, thus imposing the donor's specific values and norms. This book provides an in-depth analysis of this weaponisation of foreign aid within a framework of global disruption and ultimately concludes that the world is at a tipping point towards a new socio-political world order.

Asking important questions about the power dynamics at play within the aid sector, this book will be an important read for researchers across development studies, political science, international relations and global affairs.

Viktor Jakupec is an Honorary Professor in Development Studies at Deakin University, Australia and Potsdam University, Germany, and a Member of the Leibniz Society of Sciences, Berlin. His research focus includes political economy analysis, development aid policies, multilateralism and international relations. He has extensive experience as an international consultant for the Asian Development Bank, World Bank, International Finance Corporation, Millennium Challenge Corporation and EU and European Training Foundation, in Asia, MENA, the Balkans and the Caucasus countries. He holds a Dr. habil. from Giessen University and a Dr. phil. from FU Hagen.

Max Kelly is an Associate Professor and course director of International and Community Development, and Sustainable Development and Humanitarian Action, at Deakin University, Australia. Her areas of expertise include international and community development policy and practice. She has a sectoral focus on food security, food systems and sustainability at local, national and international levels, alongside a critical focus on global political economy of development and social justice.

John McKay is a partner in Analysis International in Melbourne, Australia, and Honorary Professor in Development Studies at Deakin University and in International Studies at RMIT University. He was Foundation Director of the Monash Asia Institute and the Australian APEC Study Centre, both at Monash University. He has served as President of the Australian Institute of International Affairs in Melbourne and is President of the Melbourne Chapter of the Society for International Development. He has a special interest in the economic restructuring of Asia, the emerging security situation and economic and political cooperation in the region and has undertaken detailed studies in Korea, China, Japan and Taiwan.

Routledge Explorations in Development Studies

This Development Studies series features innovative and original research at the regional and global scale. It promotes interdisciplinary scholarly works drawing on a wide spectrum of subject areas, in particular politics, health, economics, rural and urban studies, sociology, environment, anthropology, and conflict studies.

Topics of particular interest are globalization; emerging powers; children and youth; cities; education; media and communication; technology development; and climate change.

In terms of theory and method, rather than basing itself on any orthodoxy, the series draws broadly on the tool kit of the social sciences in general, emphasizing comparison, the analysis of the structure and processes, and the application of qualitative and quantitative methods.

Public Diplomacy and Civil Society Organisations
Edited by Ibrahim Natil

Gender-Based Violence in the Global South
Ideologies, Resistances, Responses, and Transformations
Edited by Ramona Biholar and Dacia L. Leslie

Why States Matter in Economic Development
The Socioeconomic Origins of Strong Institutions
Jawied Nawabi

Foreign Aid in a World in Crisis
Shifting Geopolitics in the Neoliberal Era
Viktor Jakupec, Max Kelly and John McKay

For more information about this series, please visit: www.routledge.com/ Routledge-Explorations-in-Development-Studies/book-series/REDS

Foreign Aid in a World in Crisis

Shifting Geopolitics in the Neoliberal Era

Viktor Jakupec, Max Kelly and John McKay

Routledge
Taylor & Francis Group

LONDON AND NEW YORK

First published 2024
by Routledge
4 Park Square, Milton Park, Abingdon, Oxon OX14 4RN

and by Routledge
605 Third Avenue, New York, NY 10158

Routledge is an imprint of the Taylor & Francis Group, an informa business

British Library Cataloguing-in-Publication Data
A catalogue record for this book is available from the British Library

ISBN: 978-1-032-53053-6 (hbk)
ISBN: 978-1-032-53056-7 (pbk)
ISBN: 978-1-003-40994-6 (ebk)

DOI: 10.4324/9781003409946

Typeset in Times New Roman
by codeMantra

Contents

1 Foreign Aid and World Order(s), a Political Economy of Crisis and Disruptors

Introduction: A World in Crisis

The world is in crisis, or more accurately crises. Ndlovu-Gatsheni (2021) argues that Covid was a crisis beyond a pandemic, being more akin to the civilisational crisis long predicted by Césaire (2000[1955]). He further argues that it was a crisis of modernity, revealing flaws of a modernity that creates problems without solutions. Covid was a multifaceted crisis, with ecological, existential and epistemic dimensions. Subsequently, the foregrounding of climate impacts and Ukraine conflict strengthens the claim that we are indeed in a context of multifaceted crises of modernity. Polycrisis has become the term to define a global malaise, where the concept of crisis or various crises is insufficient to capture the compounding nature of the interactions between multiple intersecting crises. This compounding effect, of Covid, the Russo-Ukraine war, impacts of climate change, economic shocks, reversal of development gains, deepening global debt crisis, forced migration and a raft of interrelated, complex issues, provides the framing of this volume. The differently experienced impact of polycrisis, and what is done to mitigate negative impacts, considering the role of aid, is the motivation for this volume. The complex context of shifting politics, economics and geography, and how these intersect in both experiencing and responding to polycrisis, is the focus. Overall, therefore the aim of this book is to foreground the geopoliticisation of foreign aid, as 'hard power' and beyond, thus questioning its relevance in its current constellation.

This context of multiple compounding crises, or polycrisis, is stretching the capacity of aid budgets even further to address needs. Although international development, operating within a context of resourcing predominantly in the form of financial flows (grant and soft loans), is not the solution to global crises, it is a stable source of assistance in many contexts from developmental through humanitarian. It is also a considerable driver of international economic and political policy and influence, and subject to rapidly changing global power dynamics.

DOI: 10.4324/9781003409946-1

The liberal rules-based world order that emerged after the World War II (WWII) has, despite significant shifts in global politics, enabled or facilitated an astonishing level of cooperation between 'Western' powers, led by the USA, Europe and Japan. The end of the Cold War shift to in essence a unipolar world led by the USA saw the dramatic expansion of economic liberalism, with an oft repeated cleavage from Keynesianism to neoliberalism, in the 1980s, incorporating intertwined neoliberal globalisation, and the spread of democracy. The ideological space that twinned neoliberalism with globalisation extended the reach of the USA not only economically but also strategically and politically.

Aid, and indeed development more broadly conceived, is firmly embedded in this liberal world order. The multilateral foundations of this world order, the World Bank and International Monetary Fund (IMF), were created at Bretton Woods in the USA in 1944. The global financial architecture and global governance structures remain until today. The World Bank is the largest development bank and the leading source of development and policy analysis. In other words, the World Bank maintains a powerful position globally in economic, and political policy and practice. The mandate of the World Bank is directly to promote economic growth and reduce poverty through technical assistance and financial support. The IMF mandate is to promote international economic and financial stability. It provides loans in the context of crisis and is in essence the lender of last resort (IMF, 2022).

There is a tendency to cite Harry S. Truman's speech in 1945 as the 'birth' of international development, denoting a developed and developing country schism, a Global North and Global South (Escobar, 1995; Peet & Hartwick, 2015), with the World Bank and IMF neither engaging with the development of Lesser Developed Countries (LDCs) nor engaging with LDCs in the discourse that surrounded their inauguration. This, in combination with the powerful role held by the USA in the Bretton Woods negotiations, supports the argument of Northern domination of these liberal economic institutions. Counter narratives around the creation of the World Bank and IMF argue that international development was an important consideration for the USA and other northern countries, and that 'southern' representatives did play a reasonable role in these deliberations, particularly Latin America, and that notably the second largest delegation at the Bretton Woods meeting was from China. What was acceptable in this specific point in time (with many of the Global South still colonies) is complex, yet the power of the USA, and the 'embedded liberalism' (a term coined by Ruggie, 1982), is clear. This embedded liberalism was argued by Ruggie (1982, 1992) to embed the global market in shared social values and institutional practices. In the context of the emergence of the global governance model of the Bretton Woods institutions, despite some descending voices, and the undeniable sway of the USA, there appears to have been some common shared values.

This, in some ways, speaks to Ruggie's (1994: 553) articulation of a pure form of multilateralism:

> ...in its pure form a multilateral security order would entail equal protection under a common security umbrella – an arrangement typically referred to as collective security. ... The counterpart principle in economic relations prescribes an international economic order in which exclusive blocs or differential treatment of trading partners and currencies are forbidden, and in which point-of-entry barriers to transactions are minimized. A commitment to national self-determination and universal human rights rounds out the pure form of the multilateralist vision.

The form of multilateralism that emerged from Bretton Woods closely resembled the US vision of a world order. Undoubtedly the multilateral form would have been significantly different if Europe, the then UUSR, or other players had been in a position of excessive power.

This division of the global into the haves and the have nots, the Global North and South, is the framing of a development perspective. The northern-centric traditional development institutions of the Bretton Woods, and beyond, including the United Nations (UN), African and Asian Development Banks (AfDB and ADB, respectively), at a high level replicate the northern-centric liberal development project. There are multiple objectives of development, the improvement of financial conditions enabling increased human development outcomes and the addressing of issues caused by underdevelopment (poverty, food insecurity, etc.), which are essentially the focus of the World Bank and other IFIs. However, responding to crises is more the purview of the IMF and UN systems. The IMF addresses shortcomings of economic and financial contexts (austerity is a well-understood term).

The multilateral development system is funded by donor governments, of which the USA has been the biggest contributor since the inception of the Bretton Woods Institutions. Of course, beyond multilateral contributions, donor governments invest through bilateral arrangements. Aid volumes, modes and geographic focus are subject in many ways to the interests of the donor nations. The relationship between aid, development and geostrategic influence is therefore clearly apparent, but equally complex. In the intervening nearly 80 years since the emergence of the modernist development project at Bretton Woods, the question of power, politics and economics, both driving global governance and responding to changing circumstances, mainly the shift from a bipolar world to a unipolar world, to a multipolar world, and in the shift from Keynesianism to neoliberalism, provides challenges. Within this system, it could be assumed that crisis is by definition a deviation from a state of non-crisis, thus abnormal and requiring intervention of those with power and capacity to address the crisis, through a US-centric vision of a better society, enacted through existing or traditional global governance models. In the post-Cold War era, although this narrative may never have held true, there was a point or peak of globalised neoliberalism embedded in Fukuyama's (1992) 'end of history'.

However, as was soon clear, the progress achieved by Western Liberalism and liberal democracy was far from the end of history. At the time of writing (late 2023) the contemporary (post-2008) context globally is framed by Global Financial Crisis (GFC), a Eurozone crisis, a climate crisis, a global pandemic, a dramatically shifting world order and a decreasing security situation with a Russo-Ukraine war, a reversal of development gains made in addressing poverty, food security and a range of associated human development indicators, drastic increases in income and wealth inequality within and between countries and a shift away from a liberal democratic ideal towards nationalism, isolationism, populism and illiberalism. The framing of the world as developed and developing is decreasingly relevant in the context of global crises, yet the international financial and development architecture remains entrenched in a Global North and Global South frame. It is almost impossible to cover the range of drastically shifting political, social, economic and other contexts which impact how attempts to address crises are designed, funded and enacted. Global governance is challenged from many quarters, not least its embeddedness in 'Northern' power holders. Yet alternative global financial initiatives and institutions (such as the China-led Belt and Road initiative (BRI) and the AIIB) have emerged, both seeking to invest and develop certain countries. Geostrategic concerns are central in a way not seen since the end of the Cold War, and development and aid are undeniably subject to geopolitical and geostrategic interests, from all quarters, traditional and non-traditional, as well as from a Global South perspective, where voice and representation are central concerns.

Acknowledging that geopolitics and geoeconomics are always present, and the demand for local, national and global investment to address current challenges, Official Development Assistance and development cooperation will remain key elements of global governance, power relations and human and planetary wellbeing, and response to crises. The relative importance of ODA and development cooperation is changing, relative to foreign direct investment, remittances. However, development cooperation within a context of global governance and political economy, and geostrategic intent is a highly relevant focus of analysis. Foreign aid exists on a spectrum from moral imperative of wealthy nations to assist other nations through to foreign aid as geostrategic and geopolitical tool, or weapon.

The remainder of this chapter positions aid within a world order deeply disrupted through recent crises in these first decades of the 21st century. It is maintained that world orders produce crises and adapt to crises by processes of regulation and transformation, imposing specific political and moral values. The multiple crises of the 21st century have different implications due to the compounding nature of theses crises. US hegemony is challenged, and economic and political stability is eroding, as is the global geopolitical system. This chapter considers the contemporary global development context, in the context of crises. The differing experiences of the Global South and Global North are considered. The chapter then briefly considers the current state of the liberal world order, neoliberalism, political, ideological and economic disruptors to increasingly contested world order(s).

The Contemporary Development Context

Post-war foreign aid, framed within an architecture of western multilateral development and finance institutions, donor governments, non-government and civil society based actors and increasingly philanthropic and private sector players, has always been a contested project, ideologically, theoretically and practically. A paradigm of international development, a differentiation between a Global North and South, developed versus developing, rich versus poor and a resulting intentional effort to 'develop' those who are underdeveloped has persisted across the intervening nearly eight decades. There have been fundamental, seismic shifts in this time, including in global power and politics and in economic ideology which, despite significant and ongoing critique, currently feels like circling the eternal cul-de-sac of neoliberalism. Shifts from an east/west to north/south framing of technological, social, political and economic superiority, and discourses on the securitisation of aid, of the effectiveness of aid, the need for good governance, the coloniality or even futility of aid, have lined a highway that has not led to western style development in most cases. The materialisation of the negative impacts of a model of development contingent on modernised 'western' vision of development increasingly challenges the economic growth mindset of human wellbeing. Planetary boundaries (Steffen et al., 2015) are becoming centralised in discourse, if not institutional change. The Sustainable Development Goals (SDGs), underpinning the development policy of traditional development space since 2015, are currently moving further out of reach.

Non-traditional donors and actors are increasingly embroiled in economic development, global governance and discourse. Most recent shifts identify the coloniality of the entrenched aid system, and a need, if not necessarily a trend, to 'shift the power'.[1] The emergence of demand-driven systems change draws heavily on localisation discourses emerging from within the humanitarian space (Kelly et al., forthcoming). This 'politics' of aid and development, in particular the vested interests of donors, recipients and the institutions and sectors that frame this relationship, are underpinned by inequalities of power and agency, issues that have imbued development theorising for decades (Mawdsley et al., 2014).

Conceptualisations of development are thus contested, related to how society understands and attempts to intervene in problems. This, of course, changes over time, and in the current context of crises, appears (although history may well tell a different tale) at a point of significant flux, in development discourse and practice. A macro historical approach has been frequently adopted in analysing challenges to development aid and dominant paradigms. At a meta-theoretical level paradigmatic shifts can be found, for example, between and within Monetarist orthodox and Marxist heterodox economics (cf. Dow, 2011), and paradigms of power relationships within and between donors and recipients (cf Rist, 2003; Hettne, 2010; Pieterse, 2010; Peet & Hartwick, 2015; Carmody, 2019).

Mainstream development discourse (discursive, normative and institutional) is framed squarely within the capitalist economy, and since the 1980s within a neoliberal (late stage) capitalist development sphere. The interlinkages between economic ideology and political/power theories became central in considering the many paradoxes of capitalism, in particular uneven development. There are two distinct crises associated with global capitalism: the first is the simultaneous creation of wealth and poverty, and the second is the ecological crisis. Amins (1974) work highlighted the relevance of the polarising nature of global capitalism, in the context of development, although notably his later work went beyond core periphery models, arguing for thinking structurally, about the global structures that reproduce Eurocentric prejudice and thus imperialist and racist foundations of capitalist system (Ndlovu-Gatsheni, 2021). Capitalism is indeed the epitome of paradox, not only demonstrating a tendency towards crisis, change and instability but also having an ability to stabilise institutions, rules and norms. Inequality and planetary ecological crisis predominantly the impact of a changing climate are two consequential outcomes of this. Piketty (2020) argues a clear link between colonial domination and appropriation, the rise of a private ownership society and the extreme and rising inequality of the present.

The unevenness (Harvey, 2006) of modernistic, capitalist development requires and is subject to political economy analysis. A political economy of aid must, as Büscher[2] (2019) argues, not only consider the 'extreme volatility in contemporary political economic fortunes across and between spaces of the world economy' (Harvey, cited in Büscher (2019: 485) but must also consider theorisations of development. To deeply engage in political economy of development therefore also must position debates in historical and geographical contexts. In the current development settings, issues of geopolitics and geoeconomics are central. The rationale for the giving and receiving of aid is much more complex than a general intent to help, or the headline of a general desire to 'improve the lives of people around the world' (see, for example, UK Parliament, 2021). Aid is inherently political. Woods (2005) in analysing shifting political space for foreign aid considered there were three key challenges. The first is the goal, the second is the money, and the third is the delivery of aid (including lack of coordination resulting in competition and chaos). A foreign aid programme within a donor government is inherently both deeply political and also subject to economic ideology, and geostrategic focus, of the donor government, and accountability to the donor nation voters. USAID, for example, states that its work 'advances US national security and economic prosperity, demonstrates US' generosity, and promotes a path to recipient self-reliance and resilience'[3]. Australia via DFAT is clear about the strategic goal for Australia's development 'investments' for the national interest in security and prosperity, and to protect international rules, as well as making Australia 'stronger and more influential in the world'[4]. UKAID is a little more circumspect with strategic objectives to including 'strengthening global peace, security and governance' and promoting global prosperity as well as more development-oriented objectives.

Having foreign policy, geostrategic, economic and commercial interest as donors is not constrained to 'traditional' donors. The term traditional donor is used generally to denote donors who are Development Assistance Committee (DAC) members of the Organisation for Economic Cooperation and Development (OECD). Traditional aid flows are also used to refer to multilateral aid flows through western-led Multilateral institutions, including Multilateral Development Banks, the European Commission, UN organisations. Therefore, all donors and institutions that fall outside this are referred to as 'new', 'emerging', 'non traditional' or 'other' donors, and this includes all non-DAC[5] members, of which the major are the Peoples Republic of China (forthwith China), the United Arab Emirates (UAE), Saudi Arabia and Turkiye. The UAE government website makes a bold claim that 'The UAE's aid has only humanitarian objectives. It is neither governed by politics nor is it limited by geography, race, colour or religion of the beneficiary'[6].

China has emerged as a major world power, leading to a shift from a unipolar (USA) world to a bi- or multipolar world. China is the subject of considerable analysis with regard to its global investments through the BRI, its investments through development cooperation and its geostrategic goals, explicit in intentions to take an active part in global governance. Yuan et al. (2022) highlight key aspects of increasing Chinese engagement with development assistance and foreign aid, namely, the policy of non-interference, lack of conditionalities and a focus on hard infrastructure. They note the clear mandate for Chinese development investments to serve foreign policy and commercial interests with a view to increasing power in international affairs (Yuan et al., 2022). There is considerable debate around the politicisation of Chinese lending under the banner of 'debt trap diplomacy' (Chellaney, 2017). The contested charge of predatory lending has been levelled primarily at China (Parker & Chefitz, 2018). Brautigan and Rithmire (2021) argue media hype about Chinese creating debt traps as a precursor to seizing assets in recompense for unmet debt repayments is a narrative that is simplistic, unsupported and weaponised by many. The discourse around the BRI has become a powerful weapon in geopolitical discourse and strategy, both from those seeking to fearmonger Chinese geopolitical pursuits through global investments and from those who see Chinese investments as no more problematic than other lending, in the context of current global economic and political conditions. Within this complex and contested development context, this chapter now turns to notions of crisis.

Crisis, Polycrisis and Permacrisis

Crisis conceptually is debated across a range of disciplines. With origins in Ancient Greek referring to a time of decision-making or judgement, crisis according to Anthropologists, Henig and Knight (2023) is a fleeting rupture in the normal or expected progression of things.

Hermann's (1969) work within International Relations is highly influential in conceptualising crisis and non-crisis periods, primarily from a decision-making perspective, asking what are the impact(s) of crisis on decision-maker behaviour. Herman viewed crisis as time determined, unanticipated and perceived threat level by the decision-maker. Hermann's work is theoretical, in that it does not identify specific substance of subject as crisis. Against this more procedural approach, Phillips and Rimkunas (1978) contrast a substantive approach which is specific to the content of a particular situation.

Crisis from an IR perspective focuses on state and behaviour, with Phillips and Rimkunas (1978) noting some general agreement on unusual, or difficult to forecast, forms of behaviours, a shift in modes of behaviours from pre-crisis standard operating procedures to crisis response. They argue that threat is the driving variable defining crisis behaviour. Hermann's later work reconsidered the surprise factor, moving from notions of crisis as unanticipated to uncertain, with escalation and/or a combination of factors coalescing to create threat.[7] States were the only crisis actors initially (Hermann, 1969; Brecher, 1993). However, Brecher (1993) among others broadened the debate to consider systemic crisis, such as crisis in the international system, and disruptive interactions among nations, accompanied by shifts within the international system, including power shifts, norms, rules or shifts in key actors.

Henig and Knight (2023) consider crisis as more than a transitory state. Arguably, in historic context crises were the norm. Just in the 20th century it is impossible to cover the full range of crises, WWI and II, the Cold War, Nuclear threats, USSR invasion of Hungary in 1956 Czechoslovakia in 1968, 1979 invasion of Afghanistan, the Berlin Blockade (1948–1949), the Cuban Missile Crises (1962), the complexities of 20 years of the Vietnam War, the Korean War, the Suez Crisis, the 1970s Energy Crisis, Spanish Flu, HIV/Aids, Cholera, Rwandan Genocide, September 11th attack on the USA and resulting USA involvement in Afghanistan, the war on terror and the various wars in the Middle East and North Africa, among many other crises. If one considers post-WWII wars and political, economic, financial and military crises it can be shown crises as the normal state. Many of these crises were largely contained within specific countries and regions or geopolitical spheres of interests. Yet Vigh (2008) argues that there is dissonance between debates on crisis for a significant number of people for whom crisis is neither temporary nor aberrant, but endemic. The privileged position that considers peace and prosperity as the baseline ignores the lived experience of the socially marginalised, structurally violated or poor (Vigh, 2008). Development assistance is predicated on those for whom crisis is endemic.

The current crises are centred on crises that are now planetary in nature, where complexity and systems are challenged, not just to the detriment of those previously marginalised but encompassing those who are used to being in a position of power, wealth and peace (the Global North). Adam Tooze has become a central figure in debating the current state of the world, popularising the notion of polycrisis, in an opinion piece in the *Financial Times*[8] It seemed to hit a nerve,

> A problem becomes a crisis when it challenges our ability to cope and thus threatens our identity. In the polycrisis the shocks are disparate, but they interact so that the whole is even more overwhelming than the sum of the parts. At times one feels as if one is losing one's sense of reality.
>
> (np)

This notion of polycrisis is used as a narrative device to explain a kind of collective unease, or malaise. The World Economic Forum (2023) drew heavily on the notion of polycrisis, defined as a phenomenon '…where disparate crises interact such that the overall impact far exceeds the sum of each part' (World Economic Forum 2023: np), to contextualise their World Risk Report for 2023. Polycrisis sits alongside or indeed possibly even contradicts 'permacrisis'[9] defined as an extended period of instability and insecurity.[10] The question is whether a permanent state of crisis is in fact even possible or whether it is better conceptualised as representing a new state. Turnbull (2022) debates the notion that a crisis can be linked to a turning point, or a transition to a future state, which can be positive, such as Kuhn's paradigmatic shifts, or become embedded, such as Marx and the crisis of capitalism. However, he argues it is the link between systems thinking and crisis where permacrisis exists, when crises become so complicated that it is not possible to predict the outcome. Henig and Knight (2023: 3) in considering the purpose of a word such as polycrisis come to the conclusion that:

> …polycrisis adds a layer to the crisis trope for seeing the world through a lens of what we suggest calling knotted eventedness. It provides an alternative narrative angle to draw attention to domains of meaning, causalities

and the socio-political need to act. The original rupture of crisis as a time of judgement or decision- making may not be immediate and instead engenders new rhythms and entanglements with longer-term temporalities.

Henig and Knight (2023) raise the spectre that even if we concur that we live in a very new context, of climate crisis, there are questions as to what constitutes a polycrisis relevant to this moment, more so than other historical moment. They refer to the great acceleration of the post-war era, which may be considered the root of these crises, or the crisis of capitalism, or, in fact, Ndlovu-Gatsheni's (2021) crisis of modernity.

Development assistance has been based on a project of modernisation, yet the current crisis deepens the critique of modernisation paradigm, of the superiority of the Northern vision of development. Late stage capitalism is widely agreed to be central to the evolution of the current context of a polycrisis in a number of claimed ways. Plys (2014) in an analysis of interrelationships between crisis, profits and financialisation positions her research centrally within notions of capitalism, and (economic) crisis, thus:

> Central to the historical development of capitalism is crisis: a moment of change from one way of organizing the economy to another, from one accepted political order to another, and from one set of dominant ideas to another. Understanding these transitional moments helps us understand how and why our contemporary world-economy takes the form that it does. If we can understand how economic, political, and ideological power is constructed over time.
>
> (Plys, 2014: 24)

The central role of the "American Empire' and its institutional support for the predominance of capital over labour, Panitch and Gindin (2012) argue, both complicate a linear narrative of economic liberalism and lay firm foundations for the dominance of global corporations, based on concentration of funds through the perceived reputation of Wall Street. However, it also cemented the 'Americanisation' of Western Europe and Japan, leading to a US domination of global capital, and thus corporate global capitalist economy. This argument provides a clear narrative around the threats to this global capitalist system from labour rights, nationalism and protectionism. Neoliberalism from this perspective can be a political response to counter the democratic gains made by labour through working-class actions, and which are, from the position of neoliberal purists, in fact just a barrier to capital accumulation.

Panitch and Gindin's (2012) rather detailed narrative of the relationship between global capitalism, neoliberalism and the USA provides an excellent jumping off point for consideration of international development policy and practice, and specifically aid as both economic and political tool. The USA is the biggest donor in the post-war era. The centring of American hegemony to the turn of the 21st century economically and politically in the 'West' was the foundation of international development. The framing of the 'Third World' as requiring the application of and expansion of US hegemony through trade, globalisation and democracy has been both the guiding principle of international development mainstream thought and has also been subject to considerable critique (see Chapter 4). Global governance structures (IMF and World Bank) built from post-war alliances between the USA and Western Europe were the global vehicle for the dissemination of an Americanised development model, rather simplistically but powerfully encapsulated in a modernisation paradigm, whereby LDCs could be industrialised as per Rostov's stages of growth, from traditional societies to an age of high consumption.

Multilateralism, the predominant approach to global governance, is an important but again significantly contested approach. Ruggie (1992) notes the benefits of a multilateral approach with regard to reducing interethnic rivalry between voters and support for their homelands, in the disbursement of development assistance. In essence multilateralism 'favoured everybody's homeland'. This fundamental concept is important in considering shifting geopolitical and geostrategic interests. Ruggie's 'pure' form of multilateralism would indeed provide assistance based on need. However, bilateral aid is significantly more subject to political and power distortion as the country-by-country allocations of aid are complex, and potentially highly divisive (Chapter 4). A key point of contention within the multilateral space, and one that is raised increasingly regularly, is representation. The current context is the emergence of new forms of multilateral institutions, driven from the Global South. Whether there is the capacity for convergence between these diverse organisations, bilateral donors, private sector and philanthropists in responding to global crisis, working towards economic, social and political stability (whatever this looks like) is unclear at best. Before considering these issues in more detail, this chapter now turns to issues of crisis and neoliberalism.

From Neoliberalism to Crisis to Development

Neoliberalism is the hegemonic political and economic dogma with many faces which traverses political, economic and socio-cultural dimensions. It emerged in the 1930s and 1940s and became concomitant with *laissez faire* economics (Orlowski, 2012) and a variety of subsequent interpretations and modifications. The evolution of neoliberal doctrine, or what Tribe (2021: 8) terms its 'intellectual backbone', given shape by the Mont Pellarin Society, over the intervening years enabled neoliberalism to flourish in the 1980s as flaws in Keynesianism paved the way for a new economic ideology. Chapter 2 delves into neoliberalism in more detail, but the key tenets of neoliberalism must be understood as a basis for broader contextualisation of crisis, aid and development.

The common philosophy of neoliberal schools of thought is two-fold. First, the free market acts as a universal organisational model and all aspects of life are subject to the laws of free market, thus transforming individual actors into a market domain, as unattached players, driven by self-interest, and the accumulation of resources. From this perspective, the goal of neoliberalism is to ensure the existence of a human society in which all actions between individuals, organisations and other actors are competition-based market transactions, a position that is clearly at odds with society as a relational, reciprocal space based on justice, equality and moral transactions. Issues concerning neoliberalism and social policy focus on antagonism towards the welfare state and all its materialisations, diversities and 'isms' such as collectivism. In essence welfare state ideals, from a neoliberal perspective, destabilise free-market rules, and claims for social justice restrict the neoliberal right to unrestricted wealth creation. Altruistic foreign aid and the solidarity of foreign aid donors are thus feeble collective parochial activities. Simplistically, neoliberalism is portrayed as market fundamentalism, including trade liberalisation, liberalisation of foreign direct investment, privatisation of state enterprises, infrastructures, social and health services, market deregulation, property rights and the restraint of fiscal policy. It includes redirection of public-spending subsidies towards broad-based social services investment and globalisation. The term Washington Consensus was coined by John Williamson in 1989 to refer to market-oriented policy prescriptions promoted by not only 'Washington'-based institutions but also the World Bank and IMF in the development space (Williamson, 2003), and the implications of the Washington consensus are unpacked in Chapters 2 and 4.

Neoliberalism is a form of capitalism independent of social, cultural and political inhibitions and social consciousness (Hayek, 1971, 1979; Friedman, 1976). Foreign aid is a traditional vehicle to counteract the impacts of failures of neoliberalism, to counter market failure, built on economic, social, political and development objectives, as determined by key donors. After decades of discontent, and controversy as to the effectiveness of aid at the macroeconomic level, there is some consensus that foreign aid does promote aggregate economic growth (Arndt et al., 2016), recognising that aid is not the key driver of development (Alesina & Dollar, 2000).

The reversal of development gains that characterise the development context of 2023 is now widely understood. The 2022 Human Development Report (UNDP, 2022) for the first time reported a two year decline in the Human Development Index (HDI), now back to 2016 levels. This HDR report focuses on uncertainty, unsettlement and a transforming world, the 'troubling manifestation of an emerging, new uncertainty complex' (p. iv) resulting from many challenges that are no longer clearly separate. The report predecessors focused on the climate crisis, preceded by inequality, both of which are incorporated in the 2022 analysis as interlinked and compounding.

Differentiated Impact of Crisis in the Global North and Global South

Neoliberal models of development within a global 'unleashing' (Neilson, 2020: 86) of capitalism are core to any debate on crises. The 2008 Global Financial Crisis highlighted or brought to the fore the failures of capitalism to maintain stability. Uneven development, ecological crisis and what Neilson (2020) refers to as regressive nationalism are further outcomes of a failed neoliberal project. However, as Piketty (2020) summarises, the current period of hypercapitalism is beset by many issues, particularly income inequality. A resulting difficulty is the need to take account of environmental inequalities, as both the production and consumption of carbon must be taken account of in. There is an excessively high concertation of the highest emitters in the USA. Equally, the 10% of the world highest emitting population emit 45% of global emissions (Piketty, 2019: 666).

Political narratives around climate change are intriguing. Scientists have, with increasing urgency over 35 years, been warning of the crisis embedded in the dramatic rise of Greenhouse Gases, resulting from burning fossil fuels, as well as other changes ushered in through the industrial revolution. The 2015 Paris Climate Agreement was to keep global warming below 2°, but to aim for 1.5°C, requiring significant change to standard human development approaches, reducing and phasing out fossil fuels, among other changes. The 2021 COP in Glasgow recommitted to turning the 2020s to the decade of climate action, to keep global warming below 1.5°C, a target that is increasingly unlikely to be met. The political will to address this global issue, requiring ideological, economic and political transformations, seems even further out of reach. COP 27 in Dubai, in 2022, was subject to the lobbying of the more than 600 fossil fuel lobbyists. No end to the use of coal was agreed, no mention of oil or reduced commitments to low carbon energy systems. This issue sits at the heart of the current polycrisis, and is an matter of politics and economic interests, requiring as UNFCC highlights '*economic and social transformation*'[11], a transformation that would require a reordering of power and control, globally with particular relevance to both the power of global corporations and a multilateral system that has power to enact change.

Climate, as Andrew Harper, the UNHCR special advisor on Climate Action, argues, is the defining crisis of our time. Slim (2023) highlights that the climate emergency is in fact not just one of a list of cross cutting issues to be dealt with but intersects with everything, and this reconceptualisation centring climate change is, he argues, a whole new paradigm for humanity. The context of rapid global warming and resultant extreme, more unpredictable, frequent and intense weather events are experienced differently among and between countries. Vulnerability to environmental hazards from climate change is differentiated through a range of social, economic, historical and political factors, operating multiple scales (Thomas et al., 2018). Perhaps one of the most complex aspects of climate change is the deep interconnections between climate change and global inequality. Those most at risk from impacts of climate change are the already poorest and most vulnerable, but who have contributed least to the crisis. In stark data, the IPCC reports that between 2010 and 2020 mortality rates were 15 times higher from floods, droughts and storms in vulnerable regions than richer countries, that climate change will put a further estimated 8 to 80 million people at risk of hunger, concentrated in sub-Saharan Africa, South Asia and Central America. Water security, already a global issue, is modelled to increase. Health-related impacts are both physical and mental, with climate-related illnesses, premature death, malnutrition and reductions in mental health and wellbeing. An estimated excess 250,000 deaths per year by 2050 are attributable to heat, undernutrition, malaria and diarrhoeal diseases alone. Poorly planned, non-climate sensitive human settlements, including informal settlements, coastal cities and urbanisation in LDCs, are increasing risks. Additional forced migration, negative impacts on economic growth, dramatic and irreversible loss of biodiversity and many other impacts are felt more acutely by marginalised or more vulnerable populations. Climate change mitigation and adaptation are essential, with significant discourse around climate finance, as one component part of global investment. Yet, even in Australia, subject to extreme weather events, 3 new coal mines have been approved since 2022, with 25 additional (new or expanded) proposals waiting for approval (Australia Institute, 2023).

Global hunger and food security is an alarming example of how some of the above multiple crises interact. Interrelated drivers of food insecurity include volatility of food prices, armed conflicts, political instability, climate change and weather events, poverty and economic challenges, crops, pests and livestock diseases. The 2023 State of Food and Nutrition security in the world (FAO et al., 2023) makes for depressing reading. Figures for undernourishment show global decreases from 2000 to around 2015, but despite some further gains in addressing food security in South Asia until 2017, both the percentage and real numbers of food insecure people rose steadily to 2020. Covid, climate impacts and the Russo-Ukraine war drove figures of moderately or severely food insecure people globally to around 30% of the population (2.4 billion people) of whom 11.3% (900 million people) are severely food insecure (FAO et al., 2023). However, reductions in Asia conceal a rise from 45% to 64% of the population experiencing moderate or severe food insecurity in sub-Saharan Africa.

The global food crisis has seen a 19% prince index rise from January 2020 to July 2023. Not only does this make food less accessible, but it also dramatically increased operating costs for the World Food Programme, in essence the place of last resort for populations in severe food crisis. Monthly operating costs for the WFP are 44% higher in mid-2023 than they were on average for 2019. This cost blowout is estimated by the WFP to equate to the cost of feeding 4 million people a month.[12] Looking forwards, modelling of the food system shows potential for concurrent crop failures in the mid latitudes (Kornhuber et al., 2023) and impacts from global trade agreements and disagreements (US-China trade war), financialisation and commodification of foods (reducing supply and demand factors), increasing input prices (fertiliser particularly) and conflict. The food system is in absolute crisis.

The Ukraine-Russo war is another central part of the current polycrisis. The current invasion was predated by Russian invasion and subsequent annexation of the Crimean Peninsula in 2014 and the full scale Russian invasion in February 2022. At the current time, there is no clear end to the war in sight. President Zelenevsky has stated that no territories will be ceded to Russia but may commence negotiations when Ukraine forces attain the border of the occupied Crimean Peninsula (Davies, 2023). Food is undeniably a political tool in the Russo-Ukraine war. A trade deal which saw a grain exported from Ukraine via the Black Sea,[13] which helped stabilise global wheat supplies and food prices and was of particular importance for Africa and parts of the Middle East, as well as the World Food Programme, has now been abandoned by Russia, a move that is cited as weaponising food (Mpoke Bigg & Nechepurenk, 2023). This was followed by a missile barrage at Ukraine's grain exporting terminals, and demands from Putin for changes to sanctions, as well as a political nod, or gouge, to the impact of the collapse of the Black Sea grain deal – with Putin claiming that Russia will continue to supply grain, food products, fertilisers and other goods to Africa (Waterhouse, 2023). Even when the war is over, the finances required to rebuild the country are vast. The implications for a significant slowing of global economic recovery from Covid-19 were mapped by the OECD and felt most deeply in Europe, with related energy crisis (OECD, 2022).

Economically, there is yet another arm to the crisis, current and emerging, framed by a global economic downturn, with global growth slowing dramatically in response to increasing inflation, and interest rates, reducing investment and factors outlined above (e. g. Ukraine conflict). The implications of the current economic context are vital when considering global development. The World Economic Outlook, in January 2023, forecasted a sharp and long-lasting slowdown in global growth that will hit many countries of the Global South hard (Malpass, 2023: np). Roughly one in five developing[14] countries are effectively unable to access financial markets, as investment and access to capital are limited through a 50 year high in debt (Malpass, 2023).

The 2023 World Debt Report from the UN refers to this as the global debt storm. The fastest growing public debt which totals almost 30% of public debt is owed by developing countries. These figures are exacerbated by the high and rising cost of external debt in foreign currency, in essence developing countries pay more to borrow. This picture is complicated further by the source of financing, with an increase in private finance. Developing countries reliance on private finance has grown from 47% in 2010 to 62% in 2021. Bilateral debt was reduced from 22% to 14% and multilateral debt from 30% to 24%, making refinancing more complex. In 2021, 50 countries were paying more than 10% of public revenue to cover interest payments. Depressingly, interest payments are growing faster than any other public expenditure (such as health and education) in developing countries. In bald figures 3.3 billion people live in countries that spend more on interest payments than on education or health.

Debt relief is therefore a point of significant discussion. This, however, is yet again embedded in complex, entangled mess of politics and economics. China has called for multilateral institutions (the IMF and World Bank) to initiate debt relief. However, there are significant critiques, given the complex interplay of private sector debt, Chinese and other bilateral and multilateral debt. As Kant noted, '*it cant be that the IMF takes a haircut, and it goes to settle Chinese debt... Everybody has to take a haircut*' (Kant, quoted by Bhatia & Wells, 2023: np). Debt is mired in conditions of inequality. It seems essential that for any realistic chance of addressing polycrisis impacts economic justice is one more essential component, requiring global commitment and cooperation.

In exploring the Covid-19 pandemic the link between differentiated experiences of crisis and the increasing impact of geopolitical influence becomes even clearer (Kelly & McGlasson, 2022). The shutting down of much of the world, and with an estimated 7 million deaths attributable to Covid-19 (WHO, 2023), is a short summary of a global health crisis. The economic interconnectedness of globalised world fell short when massive disruptions to global demand and supply shocks disrupted global value chains, through governments' policy that closed borders, halting work, socialising, in many cases education, and causing cascading effects that will reverberate socially and economically for years to come according to the OECD (2020). While the Global North was paralysed by infection and mortality rates, population movement controls and border closures, the Global South experience of Covid-19 was framed by a shadow pandemic of second-order impacts including dramatic reductions in management of other health issues. Estimates of impacts include potential doubling of Malaria deaths, 400,000 extra Tuberculosis deaths and half a million extra death from HIV/AIDS as a result. Economic vulnerability was higher in lower income countries; increased poverty, curtailed education, rising food insecurity and impacts on women and girls, the elderly and other marginalised groups were greater, as they always are. For daily wage and migrant workers, lockdowns were disastrous (Jesline et al., 2021).

In essence the crises outlined above are a tale of two halves: those with (resources to weather an adverse event, social safety nets, government capacity to borrow and invest in creating these) and those without. The experience of Covid, climate impacts, etc. is subject to the same conclusion, as is food security, access to healthcare, education, livelihoods, forced migration and so many of the interrelated spaces that surround adverse events. This is thus also, as Appiah back in (2021) argued very eloquently, a tale of two international orders.

Geopolitical and Geoeconomic Disruptors to Increasingly Contested World Order(S)

Aid is, at a headline level, intended to improve the lives of people, and increasingly to mitigate or adapt to the climatic conditions created by 'overdevelopment'. However, there is little disagreement that aid also has a utilitarian approach, used in the pursuit of the interest of the donor, through economic benefits to the donor, promotion of donors' geopolitical and geoeconomic agendas and the more nebulous intent of securing allies. Aid can therefore be a tool of development, of diplomacy, of hard and soft power, or what Nye (2017) terms, 'smart power'. He defined soft power as one component of state-level influence that can affect others through attraction and persuasion rather than coercion or payment, the battle for hearts and minds. He argued that soft power was rarely sufficient, but in combination with and reinforcing hard power could be considered 'smart power'.

The impact of the dominant political economy, and its vision of a good life, is not only domestic but, as Gerstle (2022) argues, impacts the global order as well. Reference is made previously to the neoliberal rules-based world order and the shifting world order(s). Within international relations the notion of the liberal world order is debated heavily. It refers to what Ikenberry (2018) argues a multilayered and multifaceted aggregation of various ordering rules and institutions. Ikenberry (2018) further argues that 'some of these domains of governance may have rules and institutions that narrowly reflect the interests of the hegemonic state, but most reflect negotiated outcomes based on a much broader set of interests'. As noted above, the dominant post-war world order was a bipolar world of great power competition between the USSR and the USA. With the demise of the USSR, the liberal world order of the USA becomes hegemonic. However, this is increasingly under pressure from a range of disruptors, and in particular the rise of China as a great power. Alongside the US/China competition, Russia and other countries are also vying for influence. The existing global aid and governance architecture of the Bretton

Woods Institutions are challenged by the rise of non-traditional donors and institutions.

Chapter 2 delves into more detail on neoliberal hegemony, from the perspective of foreign aid, examining the embeddedness, and persistence of neoliberalism within the aid architecture, despite widely recognised challenges and failures. Chapter 3 brings the focus back to world order(s) considering global governance, given the deep disruptions that are challenging global stability and the survival of existing world order. The chapter explores key challenges to global stability. It considers potential required reform to global governance, and institutions in light of the retreat of global solidarity and the resulting power differentials between the wealthy and powerful, and nations and individuals who do fall into this category. Chapter 4 draws on the key points from Chapters 2 and 3, to consider potential responses to past and current contexts and crises, focusing on aid and development.

Conclusion

As Liao and Lee (2022) highlight, international development sector is subject to increasing impact of great power competition. This changing geopolitical landscape creates challenges for recipient countries in navigating required partnerships with donors. It further challenges donor intentions with regard to aid prioritisation and intent. In a context of increasing uncertainty, polycrisis and increasing human, planetary and humanitarian demands there is a massive tension central to both aid and development discourse. If aid were to be utilised in a way that was principally to help (invoking some highly complex ethical and philosophical debate between utilitarianism, prioritarianism, egalitarianism and beyond!), then a return to Ruggie's (1994) pure form of multilateralism is required. Yet if, as it does, foreign aid has hard and soft power consequences, then there is scope for aid to become a political tool, or indeed even a weapon. Even more consequentially, if a donor is creating influence through aid, yet is also promoting a rule-based order that embeds inequality and suppresses capacity for power sharing or voice in determining a state's own development priorities, or refuses to engage with climate change, or creates conflict, or many other examples of acting unilaterally, rather then the system **is** fundamentally broken.

In the context of the current polycrisis it is essential to consider the exceptionally complex interlinkages between the many moving parts that make up a polycrisis (or indeed if the notion of a polycrisis helps conceptualise the current context, rather than simplify it). To consider each of the compounding aspects of the polycrisis in isolation is unlikely to provide an improvement in human or planetary wellbeing. Considering crisis, shifts in the neoliberal world order, in the geopolitics that are so prominent in all aspects of decision-making, and governance, and the role that development cooperation, foreign aid and ODA do, and could play is to consider the potential for aid to be increasingly a geostrategic tool, or indeed to become further weaponised. Providing a rationale for the importance of critical appraisal of a political economy of aid and development that is grounded in geostrategic concerns, this first chapter concludes that traditional aid donors are increasingly subject to political and economic forces that challenge a discourse of global interdependence, in the context of crisis. New donors and institutions and rapidly shifting global power dynamics require a critical appraisal of foreign aid, its drivers, its intentionality and the possibility of the futility of aid in a system that has shifted away from globalised neoliberal world order.

Notes

1 Shift the Power emerged from the 2016 https://globalfundcommunityfoundations. org/.
2 Buscher is writing here in critique of Horner and Hulme, 2019 who argue for a reconceptualisation from International Development to Global Development.
3 https://www.usaid.gov/.
4 https://www.dfat.gov.au/development/australias-development-program.
5 The Development Assistance Committee of the OECD.
6 https://u.ae/en/information-and-services/charity-and-humanitarian-work/ the-uae-aid-to-foreign-countries.
7 Hermanns later work also concentrated more on military activities.
8 https://www.ft.com/content/498398e7-11b1-494b-9cd3-6d669dc3de33.
9 Collins Dictionary Word of the Year for 2022.
10 https://blog.collinsdictionary.com/language-lovers/a-year-of-permacrisis/.
11 https://unfccc.int/process-and-meetings/the-paris-agreement/the-glasgow-climate-pact-key-outcomes-from-cop26.
12 https://www.wfp.org/global-hunger-crisis.
13 The Black Sea Grain Initiative.
14 The terminology of 'developing' is subject to significant critique being a deficit-based, and non-specific descriptor. It is used in this context as the terminology of the report.

References

Alesina, A., & Dollar, D. (2000). Who gives foreign aid to whom and why? *Journal of Economic Growth, 5*, 33–63.

Amin, S. (1974). *Accumulation on a World Scale.* Sussex: Harvester Press.

Australia Institute. (2023). Coal mine tracker, Australia. https://australiainstitute.org.au/ initiative/coal-mine-tracker/

Bhatia, R., & Wells, S. (2023). *India Pressures China to Take Haircut on Loans to Poor Nations.* Bloomberg. https://www.bloomberg.com/news/articles/2023-02-14/india-says-china-should-take-losses-in-poor-nation-debt-rework#xj4y7vzkg

Brautigan, D., & Rithmire, D. (2021). The Chinese 'Debt Trap' is a myth. *The Atlantic,* February 6. https://www.theatlantic.com/international/archive/2021/02/china-debt-trap-diplomacy/617953/

Brecher, M. (1993). *Crises in World Politics: Theory and Reality.* Oxford: Pergamon Press.

Büscher, B. (2019). From 'Global' to 'Revolutionary' development. *Development and Change, 50*, 484–494.

Carmody, P. (2019). *Development Theory and Practice in a Changing World.* Abingdon: Routledge.

Césaire, A. (2000). *Discourse on Colonialism.* New York: Monthly Review Press.

Chellaney, B. (2017). China's debt-trap diplomacy, January 23. https://www.project-syndicate.org/commentary/china-one-belt-one-road-loans-debt-by-brahma-chellaney-2017-01

Davies, G. (2023). Zelenskyy to ABC: How Russia-Ukraine war could end, thoughts on US politics and Putin's weakness. *ABC News,* July 10. https://abcnews.go.com/Politics/zelenskyy-abc-russia-ukraine-war-end-thoughts-us/story?id=100903255

Dow, S. C. (2011). Heterodox economics: history and prospects. *Cambridge Journal of Economics,* 35(6), 1151–1165.

Escobar, A. (1995). *Encountering Development: The Making and Unmaking of the Third World.* Princeton: Princeton University Press.

Food and Agriculture Authority of the United Nations (FAO). (2023). Food Price Index 2020-2023. https://www.fao.org/worldfoodsituation/foodpricesindex/en/

Friedman, M. (1976). *Kapitalismus und Freiheit.* Stuttgart: Deutscher Taschenbuch Verlag.

Fukuyama, F. (1992). *The End of History and the Last Man.* New York: Free Press.

Gerstle, G. (2022). *The Rise and Fall of the Neoliberal Order: America and the World in the Free Market Era.* New York and Oxford: Academic Press.

G. John Ikenberry, The end of liberal international order?, *International Affairs,* Volume 94, Issue 1, January 2018, Pages 7–23.

Harvey, D. (2006). *Spaces of Global Capitalism: A Theory of Uneven Geographical Development.* London: Verso.

Hayek, F. A. (1971). *Die Verfassung der Freiheit.* Tübingen: Mohr.

Hayek, F. A. (1979). *Liberalismus. Vorträge und Aufsätze.* Tübingen: Mohr.

Henig, D., & Knight, D. M. (2023). Polycrisis: Prompts for an emerging worldview. *Anthropology Today, 39*(2), 3–6.

Hermann, C. F. (1969). International crisis as a situational variable. In J. N. Rosenau (Ed.), *International Politics and Foreign Policy* (pp. 409–421). New York: Free Press.

Hettne, B. (2010). *"Development and Security: Origins and Future".* Security Dialogue 41, no.1, 31–52.

IMF. (2022). The IMF and the World Bank. IMF Factsheet. https://www.imf.org/en/About/Factsheets/Sheets/2022/IMF-World-Bank-New

Jesline, J., Romate, J., Rajkumar, E., et al. (2021). The plight of migrants during Covid-19 and the impact of circular migration in India: A systematic review. *Humanities and Social Sciences Communications, 8,* 231. https://doi.org/10.1057/s41599-021-00915-6

Kelly, M. and McGlasson, M. (2022) COVAX, vaccine (inter)nationalism, and the impact on the Global South experience of COVID-19, in Jakupec, V. Kelly, M. and Depercy, M. (eds) COVID-19 and Foreign Aid. Nationalism and Global Development in a New World Order, Routledge, Abingdon.

Kornhuber, K., Lesk, C., Schleussner, C. F., et al. (2023). Risks of synchronized low yields are underestimated in climate and crop model projections. *Nature Communication, 14,* 3528.

Liao, C., & Lee, B. (2022). Geopolitics of development. In Vinjamuri, et al. (Eds.), *Building Global Prosperity: Proposals for Sustainable Growth* (pp. 23–34). London: Chatham House. https://doi.org/10.55317/9781784135508

Malpass, D. (2023). Opening Remarks by World Bank Group President David Malpass during the Launch of the January 2023 Global Economic Prospects Report. World Bank. https://www.worldbank.org/en/news/speech/2023/01/10/opening-remarks-by-world-bank-group-president-david-malpass-during-the-launch-the-january-2023-global-economic-prospects

Mawdsley, E., Savage, L., & Kim, S.-M. (2014). A 'post-aid world'? *The Geographical Journal, 180,* 27–38.

Mpoke Bigg, M., & Nechepurenk, I. (2023). 'Weaponising food': Russia halts Ukraine grain deal. https://www.afr.com/world/europe/russia-dumps-crucial-ukraine-grain-deal-as-drones-attack-bridge-20230718-p5dp0z

Ndlovu-Gatsheni, S. J. (2021). Revisiting Marxism and decolonisation through the legacy of Samir Amin. *Review of African Political Economy, 48*(167), 50–65.

Neilson, D. (2020). Bringing in the 'neoliberal model of development'. *Capital & Class, 44*(1), 85–108.

Nye, J. (2017). Soft power: The origins and political progress of a concept. *Palgrave Communications, 3,* 17008.

OECD. (2020). A Systemic Resilience Approach to Dealing with Covid-19 and Future Shocks. Available at: www.oecd.org/coronavirus/policyresponses/a-systemic-resilience-approach-to-dealing-with-covid-19-and-future-shocks-36a5bdfb/

OECD. (2022). *OECD Economic Outlook,* Volume 2022 Issue 2. Paris: OECD Publishing.

Orlowski, P. (2012). Neoliberalism: Laissez-Faire revisited? In P.-P. Kuczynski & J. Williamson (Eds.), *After the Washington Consensus: Restarting Growth and Reform in Latin America.* Washington, DC: Institute for International Economics.

Panitch, L., & Gindin, S. (2012). The Making of Global Capitalism: The Political Economy of American Empire, New York, *Verso.*

Parker, S., & Chefitz, G. (2018). *Debtbook Diplomacy.* Boston, MA: Belfer Center for Science and International Affairs, Harvard Kennedy School.

Peet, R., & Hartwick, E. (2015). *Theories of Development: Contentions, Arguments, Alternatives* (3rd ed.). New York: Guilford Publications.

Phillips, W., & Rimkunas, R. (1978). The concept of crisis in international politics. *Journal of Peace Research, 15*(3), 259–272. https://doi.org/10.1177/002234337801500304

Pieterse, J. N. (2010). Development theory: Deconstructions/reconstructions. Development Theory: Deconstructions/Reconstructions.

Piketty, T. (2020). *Capital and Ideology.* Cambridge, MA: Harvard University Press.

Plys, K. (2014). Financialization, crisis, and the development of capitalism in the USA. *World Review of Political Economy, 5*(1), 24–44. https://doi.org/10.13169/worlrevipoliecon.5.1.0024

Rist, G. (2003). *The history of development: From western origins to global faith (Expanded ed.).* London: Zed Books.

Ruggie J. G. (1992). Multilateralism: the anatomy of an institution. *International Organization. 46*(3), 561–598.

Ruggie, J. G. (1994). Third try at world order? America and multilateralism after the cold war. *Political Science Quarterly, 109*(4), 553–570.

Slim, H. (2023, June 28). Humanitarians and the Climate Emergency: The Ethical, Practice and Cultural Challenges. Global Public Policy Institute, We Essay. https://gppi.net/2023/06/28/humanitarians-and-the-climate-emergency

Steffen, W., Richardson, K., Rockström, J., Cornell, S. E., Fetzer, I., Bennett, E. M., Biggs, R., Carpenter, S. R., de Vries, W., de Wit, C. A., Folke, C., Gerten, D., Heinke, J., Mace, G. M., Persson, L. M., Ramanathan, V., Reyers, B., & Sörlin, S. (2015).

Planetary boundaries: Guiding human development on a changing planet. *Science, 347*(6223), 1259855. https://doi.org/10.1126/science.1259855

Thomas, K., Hardy, R. D., Lazrus, H., et al. (2018). Explaining differential vulnerability to climate change: A social science review. *WIREs Climate Change, 10*, e565. https://doi.org/10.1002/wcc.565

Turnbull, M. (2022, November 12). Permacrisis: What it means and why it's word of the year for 2022. The Conversation. https://theconversation.com/permacrisis-what-it-means-and-why-its-word-of-the-year-for-2022-194306

UK Parliament. (2021). Importance of foreign aid programme. House of Lords Library. https://lordslibrary.parliament.uk/importance-of-foreign-aid-programme/

United Nations Development Program (UNDP). (2022). Human Development Report 2021-2022 - Uncertain Times, Unsettled Lives: Shaping our Future in a Transforming World.

Vigh, H. (2008). Crisis and chronicity: Anthropological perspectives on continuous conflict and decline. *Ethnos, 73*(1), 5–24. https://doi.org/10.1080/00141840801927509

Waterhouse, J. (2023). Ukraine war: Russia hits Odesa after killing grain deal. *BBC News Online.* https://www.bbc.com/news/world-europe-66272001

Woods, N. (2005). The shifting politics of foreign aid. *International Affairs, 81*(2), 393–409.

World Economic Forum. (2023). Global Risks Report 2023. https://www.weforum.org/reports/global-risks-report-2023/in-full/1-global-risks-2023-today-s-crisis

World Health Organization. (2023). Covid-19 Dashboard. https://covid19.who.int/

Williamson, J. (2003). Overview: An agenda for restarting growth and reform. In P.-P. Kuczynski & J. Williamson (Eds.), *After the Washington Consensus: Restarting Growth and Reform in Latin America.* Washington, DC: Institute for International Economics.

Yuan, J., Xuwan, F. S., & Ouyang, X. (2022). *China's Evolving Approach to Foreign Aid.* Stockholm: SIPRI. https://doi.org/10.55163/WTNJ4163

2 A Critique of the Neoliberal World Order

A Foreign Aid Perspective

Introduction

Following the 2008 Global Economic Crisis (GFC), the appropriateness and usefulness of neoliberalism was deeply challenged. Arguably, the situation that followed the GFC may be denoted in Gramscian terminology (Gramsci, 1971; Stahl, 2019) as hegemonic crisis of neoliberalism. Despite this, neoliberalism as an ideology and in practice has, nevertheless, retained a dominant global position. In foreign aid, the donor institutions still dominate but they lost to a certain degree the consensus of the aid recipient countries.

Contemporary academic discourse concerning neoliberalism is characterised by competing critiques, from a wide range of academic disciplines, including philosophy, economics, education, social sciences and history. Less attention to neoliberalism as an ideology and its impact has been given by the Western-led international finance institutions (IFIs) such as the World Bank, International Monetary Fund (IMF), the European Bank for Reconstruction and Development (EBRD) and a range of regional development banks such as the Asian Development Bank (ADB), African Development Bank (AfDB) and others.

This chapter, building on the basic premise of neoliberalism contained in Chapter 1, provides a deeper analysis of the neoliberal agenda imposed by Western-led IFIs and other donors on developing countries requiring the latter to roll back the state and its intervention in the market economy. However, with the rise of competing China-led IFIs such as the New Development Bank and the Asian Infrastructure Investment Bank, the neoliberal ideology governing the Western-led IFIs is losing their hegemonic status. This is in part due to other crises, such as the European Sovereign Debt crisis (ESDC) and the European migration crisis. These earlier crises were impacting the neoliberal hegemony of the Western-led IFIs. Against this background, a brief critical discourse of neoliberalism is provided within a framework of foreign aid.

DOI: 10.4324/9781003409946-2

Neoliberalism: An Outline

Despite the lack of consensus on definitions of neoliberalism, it is important to state that neoliberalism is not deprived of theoretical bases, but that it consists of different neoliberal schools of thought, such as the Austrian School represented by Ludwig Mises (1979) and Friedrich Hayek (1944), and the monetarist Chicago School pioneered by Milton Friedman (2002). Neoliberalism is often aligned with the rational choice theory advanced by Gary Becker (1976) and James Buchanan's (1967) the public choice theory.

For reasons of brevity, only overall generic underpinnings of neoliberalism are presented. For example, the Austrian School of thought, which emerged in Vienna during the late 19th and early 20th centuries, concentrates on the purposeful conducts of individual entities. Within this school of thought neoliberalism denotes free-market economics. The monetarist Chicago School was influenced by the Austrian School and founded in the 1930s by Frank Hyneman Knight (Burns, 2016). It is based on rational expectations and focusses on the values of government non-intervention into economic, political and social aspects of a country. This includes the need for governments to refrain from intervening in private transactions. The rational choice theory school of thought emerged in the 1960s (cf. Bourdieu, 2005) and is grounded in the supposition that individual actors select a course of action which is increasingly aligned with their individual preferences, and which require the least effort to achieve their personal choices. This theory is employed by economists to simulate individuals' decision-making, particularly within a framework of microeconomics. Finally, public choice theory, with its neoliberal overtones, which emerged in the 1950s (Steger & Ravi, 2013) as a distinct field of economics, is mainly used in political sciences and government decision-making, and specialising in the study of taxation and public expenditure. Proponents of this school of thought advocate increased utilisation of private sector resources by governments to source public services.

Common philosophical foundations of the neoliberal schools are presented in Chapter 1, namely, the free market as universal organisational model, the assumption of rational self-interested individuals and a presumption of a perfect free market. With reference to the perfect free market, proponents of neoliberalism adhere to a basic hypothesis, namely that the concept of the complete and unadulterated competition is created by supply and demand. This supply-demand situation creates balanced and efficient market results. By bracketing social policy in favour of free market forces neoliberalism is antagonistic towards welfare state and all its materialisations, diversities and 'isms' such as collectivism. In essence welfare state ideals, from a neoliberal perspective, destabilise the free-market rules. Thus, altruistic foreign aid and the solidarity of foreign aid donors are perceived as feeble collective parochial activities. From this perspective, neoliberalism may be defined as a form of capitalism which is independent of all social, cultural and political inhibitions and social consciousness (Hayek, 1971, 1979; Friedman, 1976).

The ensuing generic claims of neoliberalism can be summarised as de-regulation, free trade and privatisation. In short, free trade denotes freedom of global movement of human resources, goods and services, capital and in-vestment, through deregulation or reduction of laws, regulations and barriers which restrict free trade and ensure competitiveness on the global markets. However, deregulation does not mean total abolition of government interven-tion into the market. Governments operate as mechanisms supporting private economic interests as to ensure that the required conditions of a free market such as economic competitiveness and gainful capital utilisations are main-tained. For neoliberalism to succeed by its own definition, there is a need for comprehensive privatisation of public enterprises, including services, and institutions. The basic argument is that privatised entities perform more ef-ficiently than their state-owned counterparts. The state is allocated the respon-sibility to ensure order and security, akin to the classic night watchman state (Kennedy, 2005; Booth, 2007).

Neoliberalism and Foreign Aid

Neoliberalism became the dominant ideology of foreign aid following the demise of Keynesian economics in the West, especially in the USA and the UK and their allies. With the rise of neoliberalism, the basic neoliberal foreign aid agenda was grounded in 'aid for trade' and 'trade not aid' values. Today, much of Western-led foreign aid is couched within neoliberal ideologies and is characterised by aid that is tied to conditionality, specific policy reforms or objectives, of the donor. This approach is based on the belief that recipient countries must adopt specific economic policies and political reforms in order to be eligible for aid. Both the IMF and World Bank have embedded condi-tionality into their lending regime. However, critics argue that this approach can be detrimental to recipient countries, as it may prioritise short-term goals over long-term development and may lead to a loss of control over national policy decision-making. Furthermore, neoliberal foreign aid emphasises results-based management and performance measurement. This approach seeks to ensure that aid is used effectively and efficiently by setting measur-able targets and assessing progress towards those targets. However, some crit-ics argue that this focus on results can lead to a narrow and overly simplistic view of development, and may prioritise easily measurable outcomes over more complex and long-term goals.

Proponents of neoliberalism argue that it can lead to more effective and efficient aid delivery, while critics argue that it may prioritise economic growth over broader development goals and may have negative impacts on recipient countries. Be this as it may, the relationship between foreign aid and neoliberalism is complex and controversial. On both sides of the argument there are ambiguities and inconsistencies. Thus, it may be useful to analyse, however briefly some of the major notions of neoliberal foreign aid in a little more detail, particularly conditionalities, 'aid for trade' and 'trade-not-aid'.

Cabello et al. (2008: 7) define conditionality as a '… set of mechanisms in the development policy lending that the IFIs use to impose policies, such as market-opening, deregulation or privatization, on poor countries'. Pre-1980s conditionalities were primarily economic, for example, focussing on budget deficits, privatisation and trade liberalisation, and were driven by the World Bank and IMF (OECD, 2009). This changed in 2009 with the advent of the 'new aid agenda' (OECD, 2009: 31). This agenda had its roots in the World Bank analysis (Jakupec & Kelly, 2016) which ascertained an accommodating policy environment for the IFIs. This new policy environment provided a basis for more effective aid, leading to economic growth and poverty reduction. Unsurprisingly the initial conditionalities were closely linked with the Washington Consensus (Williamson, 2003; see Chapter 1). Yet it is important to note that this close link does not infer that the Washington Consensus explicitly dictated foreign aid conditionalities, which as prescribed policies were often coupled with foreign aid loans and grants imposed by the IFIs on the borrowers.

Having outlined the general concept of neoliberal conditionality within the foreign aid arena, it is possible now to turn to more specific concepts, directly rooted in Washington Consensus thinking in aid for trade and trade-not aid modalities. For example, aid for trade is closely aligned with the free-trade ideas such as marketisation and deregulation promoting free movement of goods, services, capital and human and other resources. To a large extent free-market principles became embedded as conditionalities for the provision of foreign aid by the Western-led IFIs. Aid for trade denotes development assistance intended to help foreign aid seeking countries to advance their participation in international trade. Aid for trade includes a wide range of support strategies which can assist developing countries to overcome diverse supply-side constraints, including ineffective and inefficient institutions, and regulatory frameworks (Jakupec & Kelly, 2016) and lack of supportive infrastructure, all of which can militate against a developing country's ability to enter and engage into global trade and compete effectively in world markets.

'Trade-not aid' is the concept, that economic development is better promoted through free trade, rather than the direct and indirect assistance of foreign aid. It does, however, tend to go hand in hand with other development interventions such as General Budget Support, Programme-for-Support Financing, Development Structural Adjustment Programmes, Policy Funding and Investment Project Financing initiatives, to be addressed further in this discussion. The combination of trade-not aid and the various programmes and initiatives are designed to address basically the same constraints as found in the aid-for-trade approaches. Ideally, trade-not aid strategies focus on the importance of unlocking trade and investment opportunities, reducing trade barriers and promoting fair and equitable trade practices. At the same time the proponents of trade-not aid acknowledge the importance of facilitating a developing country's capacity to compete in global markets through the development and advancement of its trade-related infrastructure.

Both aid-for-trade and trade-not-aid are aimed at promoting economic growth and economic development in aid seeking countries. As we have seen they differ in their emphasis on the role of aid and trade in achieving this goal. However, there are some commonalities between these approaches, including (i) economic development, (ii) building productive capacity, (iii) importance of trade, (iv) poverty reduction. The potential problem is that these commonalities do not pay much attention to aid recipient country-specific political, social and cultural aspects, needs and demands. In other words, Western IFIs promote a one-size-fits-all approach when addressing a country-specific economic, political and socio-cultural conditions, premised on the belief that neoliberal foreign aid solutions will work in every context. However, even within IMF the challenges of a one-size-fits-all imposition of neoliberalism have been questioned (Ostry et al., 2016) and there is a widespread debate and recognition of potential for neoliberal foreign aid policies, especially those concerning privatisation and deregulation, to lead to greater socio-economic inequalities, a diminished access to basic services by lower socio-economic strata of the population and potentially a destruction of local economies.

A Critique of Neoliberalism: A Foreign Aid Perspective

As noted above critics have argued that neoliberal policies, such as privatisation and deregulation, can lead to increased inequality, decreased access to basic services and the erosion of local economies. Taking a step back, the neoliberal foreign aid agenda in its original form of providing aid for 'hard infrastructure' became increasingly critiqued for its neglect of aid for 'soft infrastructure' such as education and health. In response IFIs and donors expanded their aid programmes accordingly. Yet they maintained the same neoliberal ideology, which led to the imposition of the neoliberal Washington Consensus-based loan conditionalities across all sectors. It could be argued that the soft and hard infrastructure based foreign aid loans and grants did not necessarily satisfy the political, economic, social and cultural requirements of developing counties. In response and over time Western-led IFIs introduced a wide range of other types of aid. This includes, for example, Structural Adjustment Programmes, General Budget Support, Programme-for-Support Financing, Development Policy Funding, Investment Project Financing and others, worthy of some further consideration within the context of neoliberalism in foreign aid.

Structural Adjustment Programmes have been the subject of extensive critique. These were developed to reform economies through the imposition of the neoliberal paradigm including trade liberation and privatisation, and by ensuring a diminishing role of governments. The basic argument was that private enterprise approach is more effective and efficient when compared with public enterprise. Structural Adjustment Programmes emerged as a response to the oil crises in the 1970s and the developing countries' debt crisis of the 1980s. Arguably, the former brought about the most severe global recession since the Great Depression. Given that due to both crises, many world economies were struggling, phase one structural adjustment loans were implemented in early 1980. The aim was to use stabilisation as an instrument to bring about economic growth. The Structural Adjustment Programmes were implemented by the World Bank, International Monetary Fund and some regional development banks, including the ADB and the AfDB (Gueorguieva & Bolt, 2003). Structural Adjustment Programmes policies were commonly used to leverage existing debt of developing countries for obtaining more market friendly transformations. Neoliberalism gained traction and achieved perhaps its high point in the 1990s. During this time neoliberal IFIs experienced a systemic change in a form of what Jesopp (2012: 5) termed a piecemeal change from roll-back to role-forward policies introduced by neoliberal governments. This went hand-in-hand with '.... a temporary ascendance of cyclical neoliberal policy adjustments elsewhere, and continuing efforts to impose neoliberal structural adjustment at almost every opportunity in many different countries' (p. 5). This enabled the proponents of neoliberalism to argue that there is no alternative to neoliberalism (Fukuyama, 1992).This assertion survived until a number of crises were attributed to neoliberal over enthusiasm.

Over years there has been a narrative of the phasing out of Structural Adjustment Programmes by the IMF and World Bank, yet conditionalities remain central to lending, particularly the IMF, and these conditions drive economic policy decisions. In response to critiques and discontent the IMF doubled down and imposed neoliberal conditionalities on borrowers irrespective of the social damage this may cause as evidenced by various Sovereign Debt Crises following the GFC. Conversely, in response to the discontent and perhaps recognising the potential competition from the PR China-led development banks and initiatives, the World Bank advanced a new development agenda based on a neoliberal-mode social lending policy. First, the World Bank adopted a theoretical stance based on institutional economics, and second, it proceeded with modifying its relationship with borrowers, their civil societies including guidelines for 'the borrower's ownership, participation and empowerment (Taylor, 2004).

General Budget Support has been on the rise since the turn of the century. It was established to facilitate greater aid recipient country ownership over loans or grants. It has been critiqued as merely disguising new modes of conditionalities, whereby the donors maintain their economic, political and socio-cultural control over the aid recipient countries (Swedlund & Lierl, 2020). Not dissimilar to other development aid trends, the enthusiasm for General Budget Support declined. One of the reasons for this phenomenon is that notwithstanding the extensive actions to advance its operations during the late 2000s, General Budget Support provisions declined. Much can be ascribed to the response to the global financial crisis (GFC) and the subsequent implementation of austerity measures. With the rise of conservatism and classical capitalist neoliberalism there was little appetite for General Budget Support type of foreign aid by donor countries and thus IFIs more generally (Morrissey, 2015; Hayman 2011). During Covid General Budget Support rose dramatically, but has declined since.

Development Policy Financing mechanism is used by the World Bank's International Development Association (IDA) aiming to provide loans, grants, guarantees or credits to foreign aid seeking countries. Such aid is 'non-earmarked' (i.e., fungible) budget support. It is also known as 'development policy lending, for supporting borrower's targeted policy reforms'. The lending IFI supplies the financial aid directly to borrowing government's general budget. However, Development Policy Financing comes with conditionalities because each loan includes policy conditions which must be agreed to and met by the borrowing government (cf. World Bank, 2021).

Investment Project Financing (World Bank, 2018) is applied to all hard and soft sectors, including education and human development, health, agriculture, public administration, energy and transport, to name but a few. Investment Project Financing covers usually medium- to long-term 'technical assistance' of a five to ten years duration. It covers capital-intensive investments, technical service provision, institution building, community-based development, micro-credit delivery and much more.

Neoliberal foreign aid became increasingly inadequate to ensure and foster economic growth in developing countries. Post-1990s, and particularly the significant failures of early phase structural adjustments programmes, neoliberalism changed again its trajectory and introduced constructs such as public-private partnerships, state rescaling and regulatory transformation, to name just a few. It could be argued that the changing trajectory led to a failure of neoliberalism in foreign aid in the global scheme of things. It is noteworthy that following the general demise of neoliberalism as a hegemonic ideology, the 1997/1998 Asian Crisis provided an impetus for neoliberal foreign aid and its revised structural adjustment programmes. In response to other crises that followed, such as the 2008/2009 GFC, the ESDC in 2010, the 2015 European Migration Crisis, the 2019 Covid-19 crisis, the 2022 Ukraine War Crisis and the associated Food and Energy Crisis and the ongoing Environmental Crisis, a discontent with neoliberal foreign aid policies emerged in the Global South. This was to a large extent due to global political and economic instabilities culminating in uneven economic and political impact at national, regional and global levels.

Despite the failures of neoliberalism over decades and in the face of various crises, especially the GFC, the Western foreign aid agenda based on neoliberal values and norms has been 'rolled forward'. This included the introduction of new policies and supporting mechanisms by the IFIs' which were designed to ensure the continuing momentum of neoliberalisation despite the increased resistance from developing nations in the wake of neoliberal failures (Moyo, 2010; Niyonkuru, 2016), and the persistence of a principal-agent theory and practices (Milner, 2013).

The Nexus of Neoliberal Institutionalisation and Globalisation

Neoliberal institutionalisation addressed within a context of foreign aid refers to the incorporation of neoliberal economic principles, norms and values into the design and implementation of foreign aid programmes by embracing a neoliberal institutional *esprit de corps*. That is, the Washington Consensus institutions, namely, the World Bank, IMF and the World Trade Organization (WTO) (formerly General Agreement on Tariffs and Trade (GATT)), achieved their global hegemonic status. Other regional development banks such as the ADB and EBRD followed suit and became 'neoliberalised'. This established firmly Hayek's and Friedman's ideology as a basis for Western-led development banks, and like-minded regional development banks which embarked on the grand project of globalisation governed by hegemonic ambitions of the Global North.

As noted in Chapter 1, from a critical vantagepoint these institutions and other IFIs are governed and dominated by powerful countries and vested interests. Thus, the global and regional IFIs often advance the interests of the wealthy nations at the expense of the poorer developing nations. The basic critique is that globalisation has augmented economic inequality and social dislocation and that hegemonic IFIs are some of the main contributors to this phenomenon. Against this background and from a critical perspective we argue that 'Western' IFIs are the leading instrumentalities through which the universal values and norms of a neoliberal world order in the foreign aid arena are clearly articulated. These banks thus promote the global hegemony of their key players, thus defining foreign aid conditionalities. That is, the constitutive values of the Washington Consensus, such as privatisation, democratisation, free trade, marketisation, deregulation and others, became part of the conditionalities imposed on aid seeking developing countries.

It could be argued that neoliberal conditionalities as they have been articulated by the Washington Consensus institutions and other likeminded IFIs have imposed substantial economic, political, social and cultural burdens on the borrowing nations. In doing so the IFIs have instituted a kind of governance which enables them to consolidate power, by taking it away from the politicians, communities and other national interest groups representing the borrower. This may well be perceived as a form of IFIs neoliberal domination of the developing countries' political, economic and societal fabric. This brings to the fore the anarchic structure of world politics (cf. Cerny & Pritchard, 2017) impacting on IFIs.

This means that IFIs reflect the institutionalisation of foreign aid and ensure their anarchic status, enabling them to influence foreign aid seeking governments' behaviour through imposed conditionalities. If we accept that IFIs are anarchic institutions, then it is not too difficult to accept the proposition that institutionalism has entrenched neoliberalism as the political, economic and social power base which in turn led to counter movements such as illiberalism and populism. These movements intend to dismantle the hegemonic and anarchic structure of neoliberalism as much as its hegemonic institutionalism.

Crouch's 'Strange Non-Death' of Neoliberalism

Neoliberalism and neoliberal institutions have since the 1990s presided over a wide range of economic, political and social crises. This begs the question: how is it possible that neoliberalism generally and in foreign aid especially has been able to maintain its hegemonic status? Here we can turn, for example, to Jesopp (2012: 1513) who observes:

Neoliberalism has had an interesting trajectory. It was initially formulated as an intellectual-cum-political project in 1938; enjoyed growing acceptance as an economic and political strategy in the 1970s; witnessed panic-stricken meetings in New York and Washington a generation later at the height of the global financial crisis; and, most recently, seems to be undergoing a return to business as usual.

Putting it differently, the proponents of neoliberalism were, despite its failures over time, capable of traversing the ever-changing political, economic and social-cultural conditions. This enabled neoliberalism to re-emerge as a, however slight, variant of itself. However, in end effect, neoliberalism failed to achieve its own goal, namely, to become a grand project which brings about system transformation and neoliberal regime shifts (Jesopp, 2012: 1517). Nevertheless, it maintained a hegemonic status.

Advocates of neoliberalism have been able to repeatedly facilitate its continuing resurrection, even when its demise was imminent. Time and again neoliberalism rose from its ashes giving credence to what (Crouch, 2011) denoted as the strange non-death of neoliberalism. Although Crouch focuses on the failure of neoliberalism and its endurance despite the GFC and the subsequent political and economic changes, his analysis may be equally applied to other global and regional crises. Crouch's fundamental proposition is that although the 2008/2009 GFC pointed to the end of neoliberalism (Jakupec, 2017), it did not really die. The same may be said about neoliberalism following the ESDC, or the Covid-19 crises with the rise of vaccine nationalism. Following Couch's argument, it can be said that in all the three crises, and others, neoliberalism has transformed itself without changing its key characteristics and at the same time adjusted to accommodate the shifting political and economic environment.

More precisely, to use Crouch's argument, neoliberalism has in all the three cases of the above-mentioned crises been able to first emerge as a 'hollowed out' construct. This means that national governments became decreasingly influential in determining their economy, while the multi-national corporations have been able to gain increased political and economic power. Second neoliberalism became 'disembedded' by detaching itself from social values and norms and the economisation of politics. Third, neoliberalism converted to 'individualisation' denoting that individuals are progressively perceived as competing entrepreneurs, rather than embedded members of the society. In general terms Couch's argument is that despite the global and regional crises including political and economic changes, neoliberalism endures a status of hegemonic ideology in the West and beyond, but as a transmuted and adjusted construct.

Drawing together these ideas, neoliberalism is maintaining its position as hegemonic political economic ideology, which remains central to foreign aid through 'traditional' donors (discussed in Chapter 1, and in more detail in Chapter 4). This is despite the well-noted failures. It is indeed a two-way reliance. For neoliberalism to be kept alive and its policies and economics to be realised, it needs to be institutionalised at various levels, and remains so within foreign aid architecture aligned with 'Western' powers.

The Rise of Alternatives to Neoliberalism: Crises, IFIs and Politics

One of the many explanations for the hegemonic status of neoliberalism is, as noted elsewhere, the argument that there is no alternative (TINA) (Berlinski, 2011). This, of course, is a simplistic argument and is difficult to sustain, for there were at least three political movements which recently challenged neoliberalism, namely, illiberalism, populism and post-neoliberalism. Despite the various crises of the 21st century which should have challenged neoliberalism, it managed to survive as a hegemon, at least partially. The rise of alternatives may be viewed from an institutional perspective and from a political-theoretical vantage point, respectively.

From the institutional perspective the alternatives to neoliberal institutions such as the Western-led IFIs are demonstrated through the establishment of alternative institutional financing and donors, such as the China-led New Development Bank, the Asian Infrastructure Investment Bank and the Belt and Road Initiative, which are in competition with Washington Consensus Institutions and other concurring regional and development banks. China formulated the Beijing Consensus an alternative to the Washington Consensus and its neoliberal narrative and shadow of doubt was cast globally over the effectiveness of the neoliberal IFIs (Jakupec & Kelly, 2019).

At about the same time the crises cycle of the 21st century emerged. Polycrisis and the nature of compounding and interconnectedness of multiple crises, as framed in Chapter 1, have emerged as central to discourse around adapting to, and responding to, multiple events. Apart from having different as much as similar impacts these crises go to the very heart of neoliberalism as a system of economic, political, social, cultural and ecological project. Let us recap, following the GFC, there was the ESDC, followed by the European Migration Crisis (EMC), the ongoing Covid-19 health crisis and the environmental crisis, the food and the energy crisis caused in part by the Russian-Ukrainian war and the 2023 banking crisis engulfing some US- and Swiss-based banks and the effect on developing countries (Dinh, 2023).

It is noteworthy that there is a direct relationship between the GFC and the ESDC, the latter crisis being a consequence of the former. The EMC was in part caused by political instabilities and economic factors and influenced by neoliberal economic policies, whereby many developed countries prioritising economic interests over the protection of refugees and migrants' rights. From a critical vantagepoint the EMC has underlined the confines, weaknesses and shortcomings of neoliberal policies, by focussing on complex political, economic, social issue that caused migration and displacement. As far as the Covid-19 crisis is concerned, it is evident that it has exacerbated existing economic inequalities, with developing countries disproportionately impacted by economic instability amongst other factors.

Turning to the political-theoretical vantage point, three main alternatives to neoliberalism emerged: populism (cf. Norris & Inglehart, 2018; Mudde, 2004), illiberalism (cf. Zakaria, 1997) and post-neoliberalism (Springer, 2014; Davies & Gane, 2021). Here the discourse becomes somewhat complicated, for in academic discussions populism has been frequently denoted as 'illiberal' (Mudde & Rovira Kaltwasser, 2017). Yet the exact meaning of 'illiberalism' is vague and at times interconnects with other concepts such as 'post-liberal'. In essence, both illiberalism and populism critique neoliberalism for its adherence to the idea of *homo economicus* as the foundation for socio-economic development. Yet perspectives vary. Populism pursues its critique of neoliberalism along the lines of a society divided into two homogenous and antagonistic groups, namely, the pure people and the corrupt elite, respectively. Being a thin-centred ideology, it attaches itself to other thick-centred ideologies such as nationalism or socialism. Populism represents a basic challenge to the main institutions and values of liberal democracy and thus neoliberalism. Today's populism is often seen as a rejection of globalisation which is dominated by the corrupt elite and thus also against neoliberalism.

Illiberalism challenges neoliberalism by prioritising national over global interests and social stability over the free-market principles. In concert with populism, illiberalism rejects globalisation; nativism shows a distrust of elites and the political, economic and social establishment and thus neoliberalism (Zakaria, 2016). In essence illiberalism is based on the principles of the *volonté générale* (general will) of the people, rather than the will of the elites. There are compelling arguments which support the claims that increased inequalities and economic dislocation created by neoliberalism have promoted the rise of illiberal movements in developed and developing countries. Furthermore, illiberal critique levelled at neoliberalism as an ideology asserts that the latter prioritises the interests of global institutions over the needs of the population generally, and thereby weakens the legitimacy of neoliberal values and norms. Illiberal and populist challenges to neoliberalism fluctuate as exemplified by political changes brought about by elections in the USA and Brazil. In essence, illiberalism and populism have lost the previously existing political credo. This allowed neoliberalism to reclaim its hegemonic (TINA) status. However, with the return of neoliberalism the most persistent and coherent critique of neoliberalism comes from the proponents of post-neoliberalism.

Post-neoliberalism is usually defined as anti-neoliberalism, denoting a collection of ideas typified by a refutation of neoliberalism and its economic policies arising from the Washington Consensus. Thus, post-neoliberalism operates in a space where neoliberalism is able to generate crises and curiously enjoys its continuing strengths. In other words, post-neoliberalism is a generic term which includes a multitude of amalgamated configurations which strengthen state functions and re-politicise foreign aid issues without completely diverging from neoliberal governance and conditionalities (Grugel & Riggirozzi, 2012; Perfeito da Silva, 2023). Proponents of post-neoliberalism refer to the free-market basis of neoliberalism and argue that the markets are imperfect and thus there is a need for state or government interventions. This constitutes one of the basic divisions between neoliberalism and post-neoliberalism (Stiglitz & Sqire, 1998).

To restate, as an alternative to neoliberalism, post-neoliberalism should not be perceived as a specific set of policies or as a definitive ideology. It is constituted as a diverse and progressing project drawing on a variety of theories and practices, and corresponding values and norms. Some of the basic philosophical positions of post-neoliberalism include (a) economic re-regulation to address the extremes of free-markets ideologies and practices; (b) ensuring the provision of social and environmental justice and dealing with inequitable distribution of power and resources, for example, between the Global North and Global South; (c) fostering public investment and proprietorship for social services, such as health care and education as well as hard infrastructure, including public ownership of infrastructures and certain industries; and (d) guaranteeing participatory democracy enabling individuals' increased control of the economic, political and social systems. This means that the proponents of post-neoliberalism argue in favour of a political will and economic sustainability which empowered governments to increase the authority of the state, and provide government-managed social and other services.

The De-hegemonisation of Foreign Aid: Some Basic Considerations

In this discussion the concept of 'hegemony' is used to denote international leadership exercised by one political entity, in our case the particular grouping of IFIs, whereby the replication of dominance includes the admission of other, less powerful entities formed by differing degrees of consensus, the persuasive use of soft power (Nye, 1990) and subsequent political legitimacy (Soull, 2010). IFIs thus become hegemons and provide foreign aid under the conditions that the weaker entity, in this case the aid seeking country's political, economic and social fabric, should be reproduced in the image of the stronger party.

Looking at the various crises of the 21st century, there are numerous indicators pointing to a de-hegemonisation of the existing, unipolar, USA-led world order and their IFIs. It would be tempting to discuss the impact of GFC on the global hegemon structure, and thus foreign aid, but this debate has been rehearsed by many others and does not need to be reiterated in much detail again. Thus, it should suffice to say that following the GFC the USA-led hegemonic block does no longer have the global power and political and economic influence it had following the dissolution of the USSR. After the GFC the USA-led unipolar world order was increasingly replaced by a bipolar world order. The GFC passed, yet despite some optimism, mainly in the camp of the orthodox economists, the world is now facing as series of novel, and compounding crises, from Covid and beyond, and the impacts on neoliberalism and foreign aid institutions are worthy of consideration.

Each of the preceding crises had the potential to bring about the de-hegemonisation of the USA-led neoliberal foreign aid agenda. For example, in the wake of the GFC, the PR China has with its state-linked foreign aid agencies provided substantial foreign aid to the developing countries in Africa, Latin America and Asia. PR China became during and following the GFC an important resource for loans. It made funding available to developing countries which were unable to obtain aid from Western IFIs. During the GFC, PR China provided over USD 75 billion in aid for energy transactions to

Eurasian countries such as Russia, Kazakhstan and Turkmenistan, and Latin American countries such as Venezuela Ecuador and Brazil, to name but a few.

To take the Covid-19 pandemic as another example there was an uncoordinated reaction leading to economic downturns, the emergence of national politics and the reinforcement of national borders. All this points to a decreasing cooperation and an increasingly fragile international system. This was underscored by the Trump's 'America First' policies and the USA's retreat from the status as a global hegemon. Even before the Covid-19 pandemic, but with reference to GFC the Trump administration habitually criticised the value of alliances and institutions, such as the WHO, NATO, the World Bank and other IFIs. The emergence and distribution of Covid vaccines by Russia and China created significant impact geostrategically (Kelly & McGlasson, 2022), given the failures of vaccine equality globally. These factors have no doubt had the hallmarks of a potential de-hegemonisation of the Western-led institutions (Norrlöf, 2020).

The crises that have emerged and solidified in the first two decades of the 21st century are continuing to have every potential to de-hegemonise foreign aid, and they did so to some extent through the various PR China development aid instrumentalities. But as on previous occasions, the Western neoliberal IFIs are continuing to reinvented themselves, and continue to co-exist in a bipolar environment in parallel to the PR China-led AIIB, NDB and the BRI initiative. Western neoliberal IFIs arguably shape shifted to be post-Washington Consensus institutions and were in competition with the Beijing Consensus (Jakupec & Kelly, 2019). This competition facilitated the emergence of a bi-polar world, which over time may bring down or limit the neoliberal project and replace it with alternative political, economic and social structures. This does not mean that neoliberalism will disappear from the world political, economic and social stage, but it may well lose its hegemonic status and become just another 'ism'. The question thus is how the Western-led neoliberal IFIs may lose their hegemonic status?

To respond to this question, it should be noted that the various global crises of the 21st century are indicators of a potential demise of the neoliberal world order, and thus the hegemonic status of Western-led IFIs. But more importantly, PR China and the Russian Federation have created new international and regional foreign aid institutions which exclude the USA and the West more generally. How far this will end the USA-led domination of global IFIs is difficult to predict. However, South-South cooperation, and China-led foreign aid, with its lack of corresponding conditionalities, has been attractive to developing countries as an alternative to the neoliberal Washington Consensus-based foreign aid offered by the USA and its allies. How this will play out moving forward, given the substantial slowing down of the Chinese economy, is discussed in more detail in Chapter 4.

Unquestionably, some of the above challenges to the USA-led neoliberal foreign aid agenda will fluctuate according to the changing political disposition of the individual aid seeking country. However, the increase of alternative lenders appears now to be a permanent feature of foreign aid. Countries of the Global South may have now much more room to move. Even if aid seeking nations do not actively change their preferred IFIs the potential that they can do so affords them with greater leverage and a stronger negotiating basis. In other words, PR China and the Russian Federation have the scope to contest the USA and its allies' hegemony and to develop alternative foreign aid world orders, which in turn have the potential to de-hegemonise the Western neoliberal foreign aid instrumentalities.

The discussion has focussed on two main crises of the 21st century, namely, the GFC and the Covid-19 pandemic. A third large crisis, the Russo-Ukraine war is an ongoing crisis, with uncertain outcomes; therefore, it may be premature to provide an analysis (Jakupec & Kelly, 2023). Whichever way this crisis may end, it will require a huge amount of foreign aid to re-build Ukraine. There are substantial questions as to who is likely to fund this. As it stands there is an unease emerging in Europe, especially within the NATO countries, where there are the first signs of popular discontent, and questions are being raised as to who will be paying, and how will Ukraine repay the loans. If the discontent amongst the population of various European Union and NATO countries and perhaps the USA with a Republican presidency and a stronger Republican Congress and Senate gains traction, we may well see the end of the USA-led hegemony at least as foreign aid is concerned. This in turn may lead to a rise of alternatives to neoliberalism in foreign aid at institutional and ideological levels.

Conclusion

It has been argued that neoliberalism is currently the globally dominant geo-economic paradigm, which has been delineated as an ideological monoculture. This means that with all its shortcomings and its ability to rise from its own ashes, its proponents have one and the same response to their critics, namely there is no alternative (TINA) (Palley, 2022). As such neoliberalism can be viewed as a hegemonic orthodoxy, namely, a mainstream global development and foreign aid policy (Tribe, 2020; Walters, 2020). Thus, neoliberalism may be perceived as the utmost radical 'ism', for it delineates the politics, economics and society as being endogenous, in relation to the free-market ideology.

However, a cautionary note is here in place, namely from an historical, political, institutional and organisational vantage point neoliberalism means different things at different times in different places (Birch & Springer, 2019). With this in mind, it could be argued that neoliberalism is characterised by a theoretical and epistemic vagueness. In short, this vagueness has led to an overabundance of theoretical discourses, epistemic concepts, delineations and analyses of neoliberalism. If this stands to reason, then the failures of neoliberalism are endemic, and unaddressable (Birch 2017; Venugopal, 2015). The capacity of neoliberalism to endure appears to be a factor of several variables. These include the lack of a clear alternative as a defining argument, the ability of neoliberal thinking to evolve and adapt, without letting go of the fundamental driver, centring the market over society and the institutionalisation of neoliberalism in global financial institutions.

As far as foreign aid is concerned, neoliberalism embraced the illusion that a strengthened globalisation can be equated to economic, political and social development, for these two constructs are seen as indivisible sides of the same righteous coin. Consequently, instead of acknowledging that developing countries would benefit from relevant targeted policies, which in turn would limit their national liability vis-à-vis the forces of global markets through protectionism, neoliberal IFIs claimed that since global free-market forces encapsulate both the means and the required ends of foreign aid development, the singular feasible foreign aid policy objective was to enact whatever policies are necessary to ensure that developing countries accept the neoliberal global requirements.

If the presented assessment of neoliberalism stands to reason, it follows that neoliberal foreign aid policies and practices were at times radical, illusionary and dogmatic. Development policies formulated by the IMF, the World Bank and likeminded regional banks dictated through conditionalities their common political, economic and social policy to the aid recipient countries. The borrowing governments were required to do more than simply ensure that the conditions of a market society are met. This included the removal of all obstacles to foreign investment, the restructuring of the labour market, privatisation of government infrastructures, enterprises and social and health services. A 'for profit' crusade would emerge as the systematising value of social, economic and political life. This, of course, is akin to the 'trade-not-aid' strategy of neoliberal foreign aid, which usually benefits the Global North and their foreign aid institutions.

Unfortunately, such a dogmatic approach taken over decades by neoliberal-focused IFIs was always tending to create or contribute to crises, economic, social and environmental, with a direct or indirect flow-on effect culminating in other crises, such as the GFC which contributed to ESDC, or the GFC's impact on the European migration crisis, due to political and economic instabilities in developing countries. However, today, neoliberal policy makers and IFIs may reasonably claim that with their approach they have surmounted some of the preceding problems and weaknesses of the earlier development aid approaches, demonstrating once again that Couch's strange non-death of neoliberalism is alive and well, globally and within IFIs.

To conclude, the death of neoliberalism has been announced previously, most prominently following the GFC. However, neoliberalism emerged stronger than before. Its proponents acknowledge that mistakes were made, but with the new knowledge and experiences, following the GFC they assured the world that neoliberalism is a worthwhile project, if not the only project which will create wealth and economic growth globally and especially for the Global South. Following various crises neoliberalism seemed to re-emerge with as much vigour as the free-market narrative characterised socially disruptive policies. The following chapters consider the political and geostrategic context of global economy and whether the current context of polycrisis can indeed be the point at which neoliberalism must finally evolve, or dissipate, given the linkages between neoliberalism and the current context.

References

Becker, G. (1976). *The Economic Approach to Human Behaviour*. Chicago: University of Chicago Press.

Berlinski, C. (2011). *There Is No Alternative: Why Margaret Thatcher Matters*. New York: Basic Books.

Birch, K. (2017). *A Research Agenda for Neoliberalism*. Cheltenham: Edward Elgar.

Birch, K., & Springer, S. (2019). Peak neoliberalism? Revisiting and rethinking the concept of neoliberalism. *Ephemera: Theory & Politics in Organization, 19*(3), 467–485.

Booth, A. E. (2007). What were colonial governments doing?: The myth of the night watchman state. In *Colonial Legacies: Economic and Social Development in East and Southeast Asia* (pp. 67–87). Honolulu: University of Hawai'i Press. https://doi.org/10.2307/j.ctt6wr2vx.9

Bourdieu, P. (2005). *The Social Structures of the Economy*. Cambridge: Polity.

Buchanan, J. (1967). *Public Finance in Democratic Process: Fiscal Institutions and the Individual Choice*. Chapel Hill: University of North Carolina Press.

Burns, S. (2016). Old (Chicago) school, new century: The link between Knight and Simons' Chicago plan to Buchanan's constitutional money. *The Constitution of Political Economy, 27*, 299–318. https://doi.org/10.1007/s10602-016-9207-9

Cabello, D., Seculova, F., & Schmidt, D. (2008). *World Bank Conditionalities: Poor Deal for Poor Countries*. Amsterdam: A SEED Europe.

Cerny, P. G., & Prichard, A. (2017). The new anarchy: Globalisation and fragmentation in world politics. *Journal of International Political Theory, 13*(3), 378–394. https://doi.org/10.1177/1755088217713765

Crouch, C. (2011). *The Strange Non-Death of Neoliberalism*. Cambridge: Polity Press.

Davies, W., & Gane, N. (2021). Post-neoliberalism? An introduction. *Theory, Culture & Society, 38*(6), 3–28. https://doi.org/10.1177/02632764211036722

Dinh, H. T. (2023). *The U.S. Banking Crisis of 2023 and its Implications for Afrika. Policy Brief - N° 23/23 Policy Centre for the New South*. Rabat: Mohamed VI Polytechnic University.

Friedman, M. (1976). *Kapitalismus und Freiheit*. Stuttgart: Deutscher Taschenbuch Verlag.

Friedman, M. (2022). *Capitalism and Freedom: Fortieth Anniversary Edition*. Chicago: Chicago University Press.

Fukuyama, F. (1992). *The End of History and the Last Man*. New York: Free Press.

Gramsci, A. (1971). *Selections from Prison Notebooks*. London: Lawrence and Wishart.

Grugel, G., & Riggirozzi, P. (2012). Post Neoliberalism: Rebuilding and Reclaiming the State in Latin America. *Development and Change, 43*(1), 1–21. https://doi.org/10.1111/j.1467-7660.2011.01746.x

Gueorguieva, A., & Bolt, K. (2003). *A Critical Review of the Literature on Structural Adjustment and the Environment.* Washington, DC: World Bank.

Hayek, F. (1944). *The Road to Serfdom.* Milton Park: Routledge.

Hayek, F. A. (1971). *Die Verfassung der Freiheit.* Tübingen: Mohr.

Hayek, F. A. (1979). *Liberalismus. Vorträge und Aufsätze.* Tübingen: Mohr.

Hayman, R. (2011). Budget support and democracy: A twist in the conditionality tale. *Third World Quarterly, 32*(4), 673–688.

Jakupec, V. (2017). *Development Aid - Populism and the End of the Neoliberal Agenda.* Cham: Springer.

Jakupec, V., & Kelly, M. (2016). Development aid: Regulatory impact assessment and conditionality. *Impact Assessment and Project Appraisal, 34*(4), 319–329. https://doi.org/10.1080/14615517.2016.1228339

Jakupec, V., & Kelly, M. (2019). *Foreign Aid in the Age of Populism: Political Economy Analysis from Washington to Beijing.* London and New York: Routledge.

Jakupec, V., & Kelly, M. (2023). Ukraine's Faustian Bargain: The first 9 months of the Russian-Ukrainian War, in Leibniz Online, Nr. *48*, 3–13. https://doi.org/10.53201/LEIBNIZONLINE47

Jesopp, B. (2012). Neoliberalism. In G. Ritzer (Ed.), *The Wiley-Blackwell Encyclopedia of Globalization* (Vol. 3, pp. 1513–1521). Hoboken, NJ: Wiley-Blackwell.

Kelly, M., & McGlasson, M. (2022). COVAX, Vaccine (inter)nationalism and the impact on the global south experience of COVID-19. In V. Jakupece, M. Kelly, & M. Depercy (Eds.), *COVID-19 and Foreign Aid, Nationalism and Global Development in a New World Order.* London: Routledge.

Kennedy, G. (2005). A 'Night Watchman' State?. In *Adam Smith's Lost Legacy.* London: Palgrave Macmillan (pp. 215–218). https://doi.org/10.1057/9780230511194_52

Milner, H. V. (2013). Why multilateralism? Foreign aid and domestic principal-agent problems. In D. G. Hawkins, D. A. Lake, D. L.Nielson, & M. J. Tierney (Eds.), *Delegation and Agency in International Organizations* (pp. 107–139). New York: Cambridge University Press, 2006.

Mises, L. (1979). *Economic Policy: Thoughts for Today and Tomorrow* (3rd. ed.). Auburn: Ludwig von Mises Institute.

Morrissey, O. (2015). Aid and government fiscal behavior: Assessing recent evidence. *World Development, 69*, 98–105.

Moyo, D. (2010). *Dead Aid.* London: Penguin Group.

Mudde, C. (2004). The Populist Zeitgeist. *Government and Opposition, 39*(4), 541–563.

Mudde, C., & Rovira Kaltwasser. C. (2017). *Populism: A Very Short Introduction.* New York: Oxford University Press.

Niyonkuru, F. (2016). Failure of foreign aid in developing countries: A quest for alternatives. *Business and Economics Journal, 7*(3), 1–9. https://doi.org/10.4172/2151–6219.1000231

Norris, P., & Inglehart, R. (2018). *Cultural Backlash: Trump, Brexit, and the Rise of Authoritarian-Populism.* New York: Cambridge University Press.

Norrlöf, C. (2020). Is COVID-19 the end of US hegemony? Public bads, leadership failures and monetary hegemony. *International Affairs, 96*(5), 1281–1303. https://doi.org/10.1093/ia/iiaa134

Nye, J. S. (1990). *Bound to Lead: The Changing Nature of American Power*. New York: Basic Books.

OECD. (2009). *Shifting aid Modalities: A Brief Historical Recapitulation, Policy Ownership and Aid Conditionality in the Light of the Financial Crisis: A Critical Review*. Paris: OECD.

Ostry, J. D., Loungani, P., & Furceri, D. (June 2016). Neoliberalism: Oversold? *Finance & Development, 53*(2), 38–41.

Palley, T. I. (2022). Theorizing varieties of capitalism: Economics and the fallacy that "There is no alternative (TINA)." FMM Working Paper 76–2022, IMK at the Hans Boeckler Foundation, Macroeconomic Policy Institute.

Perfeito da Silva P. Post-Neoliberalism and External Financial Liberalization: Comparing Left-Wing and Right-Wing Populism. Government and Opposition. 2023; 58(3): 535–555. doi:10.1017/gov.2021.50

Soull, R. (2010). Hegemony and the global political economy. *International Studies, International Studies Association*. https://doi.org/10.1093/acrefore/9780190846626.013.208

Springer, S. (2014). Postneoliberalism? *Review of Radical Political Economics, 47*(1), 5–17.

Stahl, R. M. (2019). Ruling the Interregnum: Politics and Ideology in non-hegemonic Times. *Politics and Society, 47*(3), 333–360.

Steger, M. B., & Roy K. R. (2013). First-wave neoliberalism in the 1980s: Reaganomics and Thatcherism. In *Neoliberalism: A Very Short Introduction* (1st ed.). Oxford, New York: Oxford Academic Press. https://doi.org/10.1093/actrade/9780199560516.003.0002

Stiglitz, J. E., & Squire, L. (1998). International development: Is it possible? *Foreign Policy, 110*, 138–151.

Swedlund, H. J., & Lierl, M. (2020). The rise and fall of budget support: Ownership, bargaining and donor commitment problems in foreign aid. *Development Policy Review, 38*, 50–69.

Taylor, M. (2004). Responding to neoliberalism in crisis: Discipline and empowerment in the Bank's new development agenda. *Research in Political Economy, 21*, 3–30.

Tribe, M. (2020). Introduction: Economic neoliberalism and international development. In M. Tribe (Ed.), *Economic Neoliberalism and International Development*. London: Routledge.

Venugopal, R. (2015). 'Neoliberalism as concept'. *Economy and Society, 44*(2), 165–187.

Walters, B. (2020). How did economic neoliberalism become mainstream? In M. Tribe (Ed.), *Economic Neoliberalism and International Development*. London: Routledge.

Williamson, J. (2003). Overview: An agenda for restarting growth and reform. In P.-P. Kuczynski & J. Williamson (Eds.), *After the Washington Consensus: Restarting Growth and Reform in Latin America*. Washington, DC: Institute for International Economics.

World Bank. (2018). *Bank Policy: Investment Project Financing*. Washington, DC: World Bank Group.

World Bank. (2021). *Development Policy Financing Retrospective: Facing Crisis, Fostering Recovery (English)*. Washington, DC: World Bank Group. http://documents.worldbank.org/curated/en/558621648492783178/2021

Zakaria, F. (1997). The rise of illiberal democracy. *Foreign Affairs, 76*(6), 22–43. https://doi.org/10.2307/20048274

Zakaria, F. (2016). America's Democracy Has Become Illiberal. *The Washington Post*, December 29. Retrieved from www.washingtonpost.com/opinions/america-is-becoming-a-land-of-less-liberty/2016/12/29/2a91744c-ce09-11e6-a747-d030447 80a02_story.html?

3 Crises and Disruptors of World Order(s)

The First Decades of the 21st Century

Introduction

A key question for our age concerns how the global system of governance that has been in place, however imperfectly since 1945, can be reformed in the face of the myriad of interlocking and mutually reinforcing crises that have affected us in the first two decades of the century. The existing global order is in retreat, but is far from clear what might replace it in a world that is increasingly divided into spheres of influence, and with a dominant logic oriented towards the security of a few people living in powerful countries. The promise of the Sustainable Development Goals (SDGs) to leave no one behind is being relegated to the background, and the focus, at best, is on resilience – the ability of individuals, communities and societies to prevent the worst in times of crisis.

For many years now, climate experts have been warning that as global average temperatures rise the incidence and intensity of catastrophic weather events – droughts, floods, bushfires, hurricanes, typhoons and the like – will both increase, creating a permanent sense of impending doom and nothing less than an existential global crisis. Some even suggested that the frequency of serious earthquakes may also intensify as a result, shaking the very foundations of all our lives. Climate change is just one of several serious challenges and potential crises facing global civilisation, but it can also serve as a metaphor for a broader concept of a world in crisis in which serious disruptions and even catastrophes appear to be cumulative and intensifying. The apparent inability of governments and international organisations to deal effectively with the climate crisis is mirrored in failures to negotiate the myriad of other global crises that challenge global prosperity, order and even survival. This chapter will first examine a range of threats to global stability that have emerged in the last two decades and evaluate the seriousness of each and the extent to which cumulative crises seem to be developing. It is suggested that a number of these crises are interacting in complex ways that threaten to set in train dangerous cumulative negative feedback mechanisms, as discussed in Chapter 1, what is now sometimes called a polycrisis. Next, the search for some deeper

DOI: 10.4324/9781003409946-3

and more fundamental causes that can explain these multiple sources of instability and crisis will be provided. Throughout this discussion the concern is for the mounting challenges to the global order that result from domestic instability, especially in the world's most powerful nations, and increased rivalry and competition between these major powers that have produced what many regard as the most dangerous strategic situation for many decades. All of this has, of course, far-reaching consequences for stability of the foreign aid regime, with potentially disastrous consequences for the Global South, as discussed in Chapter 4. This chapter also evaluates the prospects for improving global governance, and in the conclusion offers a critical analysis which provides some markers for dealing with the polycrisis and its various constituents.

Sources of Instability and their Consequences

The sources of political, economic, environmental and financial instability and their consequences cannot be approached as singular phenomena, for these are interwoven in complex ways and dealing with each of these separately has the potential to simplify very complex interconnected issues. For this reason, focus here is on the interrelationships of these threats and crises, and how they cumulatively constitute a dangerous and unprecedented polycrisis.

Economic Instability: The Culture of Boom, Crash and Burn

In the preceding chapter, a critique of neoliberalism, the economic philosophy that has been dominant in much of the world since the 1980s, has been advanced. Many of the sources of instability in both the economies of individual nations and in the wider international trade, finance and investment systems derive directly from the weaknesses already identified. Economies in which unrestricted market forces are allowed to determine all aspects of production and investment decisions produce, seemingly without exception, sharply increased levels of inequality as well as heightened risks of crisis, while at the same time being able to generate episodes of unprecedented expansion. The gaps between rich and poor segments of society within most countries of both the Global North and the South have reached levels not seen since the last years of the 19th century, and as John Gray (1998) has highlighted, this earlier period of polarisation was profoundly unstable, and moved the world inexorably towards the horrors of the First World War.

In the current period of globalisation, one of the key components of the move towards a neoliberal agenda, some people in the developed world have become extremely rich, but levels of dissatisfaction have if anything increased, as two recent studies have explored. LeGrand (2022) has argued that since around 1870, for the first time in human history, large segments of industrial economies have left behind mass poverty and the constraints imposed by high levels of population increase, and yet levels of disillusion and resentment seem to be dangerously high. Similarly, Roberts and Lamp (2021) point out that the phenomenon of globalisation has many faces, which have generated deep-seated resentments. In what is called the establishment narrative, globalisation is portrayed as inevitable; its international specialisation and technological progress have provided unprecedented progress, yet many people are unhappy with both the direction and speed of change.

Critics on the left point to the skewed income and wealth distributions that now characterise industrial societies, with most benefits from change flowing to the top 1% of the income distribution. Given the speed of change and the imperative to adjust and develop new skills, most workers are faced with uncertain futures and yet are offered inadequate support for retraining. Multinational corporations are seen by many as the real winners from economic globalisation, but they have used their power, along with threats to relocate their activities, to avoid paying their fair share of tax. In searching for lower cost locations they have effectively pitted countries against each other, as governments are encouraged to offer more attractive incentives than their competitors.

On the right, populist narratives have channelled the anger felt by many who feel cheated and left behind by globalisations and who long to regain control of their lives. The results of such resentment, and the desire to again have access to stable and community-building jobs, can be seen in the Brexit vote in Great Britain and the election of Donald Trump in the USA. The tenets of individualism and endless competition preached by the prophets of neoliberalism have created a world that is much less comfortable for many people, and one that is certainly less stable and predictable. In the first two decades of this century, a series of major crises have erupted, highlighting and intensifying these processes that derived from the very nature of neoliberalism. As discussed in Chapter 2, the Global Financial Crisis (GFC) of 2007/2008 had a direct impact on economies at the domestic, regional and global levels, and its impacts are still being felt. The disruptions resulting from the Covid-19 pandemic, being primarily a health crisis, also had profound economic consequences as did three political and security crises: the invasion of Iraq in 2003, the ongoing war in Ukraine and the intensifying rivalry between the USA and China. Then, hanging over everything is the spectre of climate change, which is having so many serious implications for all aspects of global affairs. The economic impacts of this global and regional polycrisis have been transformational for both the Global North and the Global South, and for relationship between them.

The GFC has been described as the most serious economic crisis since the Great Depression, and the first crisis of the global age (Tooze, 2018). Its immediate causes have generally been linked to the generation, particularly within the US banking industry, of *sub-prime mortgages*, providing housing finance to borrowers who were seen as marginal in the level of deposits that they had available and in their ability to maintain adequate levels of repayment. Banks bundled up these marginal mortgages along with others of varying quality and sold them to other institutions, in most cases verified by the rating agencies as being of the highest quality assets. When it became clear that many of these asset bundles were in fact of dubious quality and levels of default began to increase, financial institutions of all kinds attempted to limit their exposure to risk by freezing their lending across the board. Essentially the financial system ground to a halt, so that even the soundest companies were unable to access credit. This description of the chain of events that brought the entire system to the brink of meltdown is generally accurate but gives us only a rather simplistic picture of the crisis and the real dynamics behind it. Since then, there has been an enormous amount of research into the crisis and more generally into the workings of a mostly global financial system.

It is only possible here to give a short summary of this large body of research and the dynamics of the system that has been revealed. In both the Global North and South, economies are now dominated by finance, through a process of financialisation, rather than what is euphemistically called the real economy. The nature of the global financial system and its operations create or at least exacerbate crises, but the policy lessons that should have been derived from the GFC and the extensive research conducted since then seem to have been only partially implemented.

It is difficult to calculate the precise contribution that the financial sector now makes to the economies of all nations, but it is certainly large and growing (Lapavitsas, 2013). The direct contribution the sector makes to global GDP is generally estimated to be around one-quarter of the total, but the reach of finance into all regions and all sectors is now so complete that this estimate does not do justice to the role that finance now plays. Like globalisation, financialisation is now synonymous with the dominant neoliberal model. Finance has always been important to the capitalist economy, of course, but until the 1970s the major role of the finance industry was to provide the means for the real economy to operate and grow through production and trade. More recently, however, finance has now developed a more autonomous role. Money is increasingly being used to generate money (Christopherson et al., 2013). Finance now impinges on the lives of everyone, and on the nature of the cities and regions of our life world. Thus, it is possible to talk increasingly about a distinct geography of finance (Christophers, 2014, 2015).

Thus, the existence and importance of financialisation is now generally accepted, but there is much less agreement on the precise nature of the processes involved, the scale at which they operate and the dynamics that are involved. Much of the literature on financialisation has anchored the analysis at the level of the nation state, and on the USA and the UK in particular, but it is increasingly apparent that these processes are essentially global in nature (Christophers, 2012). In a series of influential papers, Shin Hyun Song and a number of co-authors have highlighted the nature and dynamics of the new international monetary and financial system. The basic argument is that rather than concentrating on individual nations – what they call an 'island model' – there is a need to focus on the interlocking matrix of financial balance sheets of major international banks and some other key intermediaries in globalised finance (Borio et al., 2014). Rather than looking at the current account, which links to the goods market, one should look at the capital account, which deals with the asset market and associated balance sheets. The leverage cycle of global banks is the prime determinant of the transmission of financial conditions across borders (Bruno & Shin, 2013; Adrian & Shin, 2009). This new dynamic is problematic in several ways. There is a strong tendency for this new system to amplify both financial surges and contractions, and thus increase the likelihood of further crises. The onset of the GFC appears to support this hypothesis. Another conclusion from this new kind of analysis is that the ability of governments and central banks to contain financial crises is now much diminished.

The technological revolution that has been gathering pace in recent decades is also amplifying some of the dynamics inherent in the kind of financial system identified by Shin and his colleagues. Lloyd and Blakemore (2023) identify the transformations that have taken place in the nature of 'the markets' but argue that the speed with which these actors react thanks to the digital revolution has created a completely new dimension to the financial system. They have illustrated this with reference to the almost instantaneous reaction to the new policy direction proposed by the British Prime Minister Liz Truss in September 2022. Markets reacted within minutes, resulting in steep falls in the value of the Pound, and as a result the policies were reversed within a week, and Truss resigned after only 50 days in power. The result of this tumultuous week was a £50 billion black hole in public finances; the massive tax cuts promised to the richest segment of the population were replaced by tax increases for all and a return to austerity, with a warning from the new Prime Minister that hard times were ahead.

The financial sector is important in all economies to facilitate production, trade, distribution and consumption, but the emergence of a significant segment of the industry that is now devoted to what is essentially speculation has made a small number of people very rich but presents a serious danger to the vast majority of the population. Warnings have appeared for some time about the disastrous impacts of these developments that Susan Strange (1986, 1997) first saw as nothing less than the emergence of *casino capitalism*, but which she then labelled *mad money*, and which Satyajit Das (2011) described as *extreme money*, but there has been little attempt to put in place adequate degrees of regulation at either the national or global level, an issue which will be discussed later in this chapter.

The Global Pandemic and its Aftermath

In early 2020 a new virus began to spread in and around the city of Wuhan in China's Hubei Province, with the first death being recorded on 10 January. By March 2020, aided particularly by airline passengers moving to all parts of the world, the Covid-19 coronavirus triggered the declaration by the World Health Organisation of a global pandemic. By then, most governments around the world had enforced lockdowns of various levels of intensity and travel across many international borders was banned. Since then there has been intense debate about the validity of the health advice on which these measures were based. Did the prolonged lockdown of the population prevent more infections and death? Was the wearing of masks effective in preventing the spread of the virus? Did the virus pose a significantly greater risk to the population than the annual outbreaks of influenza? The purpose here is not to answer any of these contentious questions, but to examine the impact of the pandemic and in particular the measures that were put in place to counter the infections.

The economic impact of the virus and the measures enacted to counter it were, in many ways, just as serious as the onset of the GFC, and like that earlier crisis its economic and social impacts still exist. Stock markets in the UA suffered losses greater than those experienced in 2008, and Tooze (2021) in his study of the pandemic suggests that if the banks had not been strengthened in response to the lessons of the GFC many of them would have floundered. The initial response to this crisis in many countries was the traditional remedy of reducing interest rates, although in most nations these were already near rock bottom and there was little space for further falls, and in any case this measure was not appropriate to deal with a crisis that was, as Tooze (2021) suggests, unlike any other in recent experience. The lockdowns meant that most people were unable to go to work, and there were mass layoffs in many companies. Technological advances meant that some people could work from home and conduct some business through the internet, but many activities ground to a halt, and in particular the global supply chains that had been developed by many companies to reduce their labour costs were severely disrupted. Even within countries both production and supply chains were badly affected. Throughout the world, health services faced severe pressures, as did a variety of social and emergency services. The need, as perceived by many governments in developed countries, was to support those workers who had been made redundant, to assist those companies that had been unable to continue with normal activities and to bolster the capacities of the health and emergency services. As in the GFC, the perception that governments would intervene decisively was essential in giving the markets the confidence needed to avert further damage. Important here was the speech made in March 2020 by the Chair of the US Federal Reserve, Jerome Powell, promising that the US government would do 'whatever it takes' to support the nation. This was backed up by massive financial assistance to support personal and small business credit of various kinds and to provide credit to many large employers. Overall confidence was soon stabilised, but there was a remarkable variety in the response by individual companies. Some activities did remarkably well out of the lockdowns: for example, some technology companies boomed as many employees were asked to work from home, and pharmaceutical companies gained massive support from governments in the race to find effective vaccines. Other companies were hit very hard by the lockdowns, notably airlines and other transport businesses, arts and entertainment activities such as live music, and restaurants, many of which were forced to rely on providing take-away food.

Levels of inequality in rich and middle-income countries – already at the highest levels in more than a century – increased still further as the harshest impacts were felt by the poor and disadvantaged elements of society. Certain groups felt particularly severe impacts. As children were forced to stay at home from school women were faced with increased burdens, including assisting their offspring with schoolwork (Green, 2021; Tooze, 2021). Many children were also badly affected by disruptions to their learning and by the social and psychological impacts of being forced to stay home and indoors for most of the day: only now is it possible to beginning to recognise the nature and severity of the long-term consequences. Many millions of people died during the pandemic, and deaths are still being recorded as new waves and variants of the virus appear, but many are now dying as the result of the neglect of screening for other diseases during the pandemic, as well as broader economic and social impacts.

At the time of writing, it is clear that the economic destabilisation resulting from the pandemic continues to be serious, and these effects are interacting in complex ways with the continued aftershocks from the GFC. In the developed world, responses to pressures coming from the populist right – grievances that delivered Brexit and the election of Donald Trump – prompted a retreat from globalisation, and in particular the export of jobs to low labour-cost countries: the 'offshoring' of jobs was partially replaced by 'onshoring'. This trend was given added impetus after the onset of the pandemic when global supply chains, essential to the whole process of globalised production, were interrupted. Security of supply became a major issue in many developed countries, especially in areas such as medical equipment, medicines and drugs, and the response was to re-establish production facilities, often with government financial support.

In the Global South the onset of the pandemic was a disaster: Oxfam argued that it represented a ten-year retreat in the fight against global poverty. The transfer of jobs to some countries in Asia, Africa and Latin America, while arguably leading to various forms of exploitation, had been one way in which significant gains could be made in raising incomes for some sections of the population. More significant for the wider populations of many countries was the imposed lockdowns. In Africa, Tanzania and Sierra Leone resisted calls for such moves but in most countries sustained lockdowns devastated the large number of people reliant on the informal sector. Similarly, reductions in external demand for primary products such as oil had a devastating effect that flowed through to all corners of these economies. Many governments in the Global South tried to support their citizens by providing food, small grants and the like, but in many cases this involved taking out yet more loans and thus increasing levels of debt. The International Labour Organisation estimated that perhaps half the global workforce was put in danger of having their livelihoods destroyed by the pandemic and the economic disruptions that it generated (Green, 2021). Anger has also been generated by way in which supplies of vaccines were hoarded by rich nations rather than being shared with needy populations in poorer countries.

Threats to Global Peace and Security: The Middle East

The global economy has faced serious challenges as the result of the GFC and the Covid pandemic, but these impacts have been magnified as the result of several security crises that have also emerged in the last two decades as the result of increased rivalries between nations, and the activities of terrorist groups. Of particular importance have been the invasion of Iraq in 2003 by the USA and its allies, the civil war in Syria, the dramatic rise of Islamic State and other terrorist organisations and more recently the invasion of Ukraine by Russian forces. In addition, there is evidence to show that throughout this period the growing rivalry – economic, strategic and ideological – between the USA and China has interacted in complex ways with these other security crises and has magnified the impacts of the economic instabilities that have already been discussed.

For decades the security situation in the Middle East has been one of the most intractable and threatening problems facing the world. There is, of course, the question of relations between Israel and the Palestinians, and the search for a two-state solution, which if anything now seems more elusive than ever. The wider region has also been of enormous importance because of its oil reserves, and this was certainly one of the factors leading to the invasion of Iraq by the USA and its allies in 2003. In the early years of the new century there was much talk of imbalances of supply and demand in the oil industry, and of a more general energy crisis facing the USA, seriously threatening its security. Thompson (2022) has suggested that this was the context within which the USA decided to invade Iraq in 2003, although the justification given for the removal of Saddam Hussein from power was the threat posed by his possession of weapons of mass destruction. The takeover of Iraq proved to be much simpler than the task add reconstructing the country, which is widely seen as a disaster in development and humanitarian terms. Primarily, and because it provided the conditions for the growth of various armed opposition groups, notably the Islamic State movement, which sought to create a cross-border Sunni insurgency and a Caliphate. The US occupation also saw the emergence of the Kurds as a significant military and political force in the region, having been previously supressed by the Saddam regime, and this in turn has generated strong responses by Turkey, which regards the Kurds as a terrorist force.

More recently, the situation in Syrian has added more complexity and violence to an already potent brew in the region. Discontent with the regime of Bashar-al Assad broke out into civil war in 2011 causing many deaths and injuries and generating massive flows of refugees fleeing the fighting. Following significant military gains by rebel forces, the tide of the civil war was turned by the intervention of Russia, which put in place effective aerial support for the Assad troops. The presence of Russian forces in the region has presented a serious dilemma to the USA in particular. President Obama has previously backed the rebel forces in Syria, but he now reversed his policy, instead attempting to work with Russia to end the civil war. However, the USA was seen as losing some of its influence in the Middle East, something that Donald Trump highlighted during his presidential campaign against Hilary Clinton, blaming her weak foreign policy agenda during her time as Secretary of State. In turn, Trump was labelled a Russian stooge, and there is strong evidence that Russia attempted to manipulate the outcome of the 2016 election. The war in Syria increased the influence of Turkey in the region and in Europe, which was forced to negotiate a deal with President Erdogan to limit the flow of Syrian migrants attempting to enter Europe via Turkey.

Turkey also gained influence by hosting a new pipeline to take Russian gas to Europe, thereby reducing Russia's dependence on other pipelines going through Ukraine (Thompson, 2022). Thus, not for the first time, issues involving energy, and oil and gas in particular, have highlighted the strategic and geopolitical problems centred on the Middle East but with enormous ramifications for the rest of the world.

Threats to Global Peace and Security: War in Ukraine

The issues of oil and gas, so often at the centre of geopolitics in the last century, have also been at the centre of the steady decline in relations between Russia and Ukraine, leading eventually to the Russian invasion on 24 February 2022. Ever since the breakup of the Soviet Union, Russia had been frustrated by its dependence, for its vital export of oil and gas to Europe, on the pipeline passing through Ukraine. By 2005 some 75% of Russian exports were passing through this route, something that also frustrated consumers in

Europe held hostage to growing tension between Moscow and Kiev that cut supplies in 2006. Thus, the decisions were made to construct alternative pipelines, one in the north under the Baltic and one in the south through Turkey and the Balkans.

But there are other, deeper issues at stake in Russia's war against Ukraine. As Figes (2022) has highlighted, Vladimir Putin is a strong believer in his particular version of Russian history, one that stretches back to the 10th century and the foundation of Kievan Rus, described by Putin as 'the first Russian state' but also claimed by Ukraine as the founder of Rus-Ukraine. For the Russian President, Ukraine has always been an integral part of the 'Russian World', a 'spiritual civilisation' linking together all the Slavic nations that were part of the Soviet Union, but which now have been separated from the core of the state by 'the greatest catastrophe of the 20th Century' which saw the breakup of the USSR. Putin sees it as his mission to bring together once again the millions of Russian citizens now stranded outside Russia. Part of this narrative also has at its centre the Russian Orthodox Church, which like Russia itself has always been targeted by the West for dismemberment and replacement by foreign institutions, values and beliefs. Thus, the war in Ukraine is a battle against the decadent West, a fundamental clash of civilisational states that will make any search for a negotiated settlement extremely difficult.

The economic costs of this war, coming soon after the GFC and the Covid-19 pandemic, are proving to be very large, with impacts throughout the world, and particularly on the Global South. Before the war many European countries were dependent on Russia for at least half of their gas supplies; hence, many consumers have been seeking alternative sources of supply in part to punish Russia for invading Ukraine but also to reduce their energy costs. Market prices for oil and gas have risen sharply, and in part liquified natural gas has filled the gap, but this is rather more expensive than dry gas delivered by pipeline. There is now significantly more interest in nuclear power through the re-opening of some older plants or the construction of newer generation modular reactors. Some older coal-fired power stations have also been re-opened or retained longer than planned, adding to problems of greenhouse gas emissions. All of these impacts on energy supply have added to the inflationary pressures now facing most countries. But it is the impacts on parts of the Global South that are particularly serious. For many years Ukraine has been a major supplier of wheat, corn, barley and sunflower oil to global markets, exporting some 5 million metric tons per month immediately before the war. Markets in Africa, particularly in Egypt, Somalia and Kenya, were important, and the World Food Programme sourced perhaps half of its supplies for distribution to needy countries from Ukraine. As detailed in Chapter 1, the Black Sea grain agreement has collapsed, and, at the time of writing, it is not clear if a new shipping agreement will be reached, and other forms of transport are considerably more expensive.

The wider implications of the Ukraine war have been explored in a recent wide-ranging paper by Bobo Lo (2023), and in particular he has considered the impacts of the conflict on the global order. For some in the West the war represents a monumental struggle between good and evil, between democratic ideals and the horrors of authoritarianism. Certainly, he argues, this war is the most important event in international affairs since the breakup of the Soviet Union, and most Western leaders have affirmed their continued commitment to the liberal international order, but for much of the world – and in particular the countries of the Global South – this war is unremarkable, simply a continuation of the endless squabbles between the major powers of the developed world. Many lack any belief in the existing international order, which they argue has done little to advance the interests of the Global South, and which the rich nations simply ignore when they feel it is in their interests to do so, as in the case of the 2003 invasion of Iraq. What the Ukraine war has done, Lo (2023) argues, is draw attention to the urgent need to completely rethink the whole notion of the global order, the goals that it is designed to serve and the role that the Global South can play within it, a set of questions which will be addressed later in this chapter, and in Chapter 4.

Threats to Global Peace and Security: US-China Rivalry

Like Russia, China also regards itself as a 'civilisational state', one that is built on ancient foundations and a powerful empire that led the world for all but the last two centuries when China endured brutal treatment and exploitation by a rampant West. President Xi now sees it as his destiny to atone for these 'centuries of humiliation' by restoring China to its proper place at the centre of world affairs. This involves the transformation of China's economy, ensuring that it cannot ever again be held hostage by a hostile West. The vulnerability of supplies of oil coming from the Middle East has been of particular concern, encouraging the development of overland pipelines from Russia and the Central Asian republics. Similarly, China has worried about the dangers of reliance on only a small number of suppliers of strategically important raw materials: new sources of iron ore in various parts of Africa and Latin America are being developed to reduce dependence on Australia, a close ally of the USA. Rapid economic growth, derived from an intimate involvement with the burgeoning global market, has supplied the means to transform China's military forces: what Roberts and Lamp (2021) call the 'geoeconomic narrative'. China now has the military power to become more assertive in the South China Sea and in the broader Asian region, and for the first time since the end of the Second World War to challenge the role of the USA as the hegemonic power and guardian of the global order.

Tensions between the USA and China – covering issues of trade and intellectual property as well as a range of security concerns – have created the most dangerous challenge to global peace since the Cold War. Throughout history, when an established power is challenged by a new and rising country the result has generally been armed conflict.

Thucydides, the historian of ancient Greece, described an early manifestation of this deadly trap in documenting the ruinous conflict between Sparta and the rising power of Athens in the Peloponnesian War of 431–404 BC. Since then, such conflicts have been labelled the *Thucydides Trap*. Graham Allison (2017) has calculated that in the last 500 years 16 cases can be identified in which the rise of a major new country has challenged the position of a dominant power, and in 12 of these cases the result was war. The most disastrous example is, of course, the challenge that a rising Germany posed for the British Empire, resulting in the First World War. Is the current situation Asia a prime example of a potential Thucydides Trap, and is war inevitable? Allison suggests that conflict, while certainly possible, need not be inevitable; however, Richard McGregor (2017) has suggested that the current situation is extremely dangerous. The USA has in Asia underwritten perhaps the most dramatic economic transformation in human history, he argues, but it has also exacerbated a toxic rivalry between China and Japan that has existed for centuries. As a result, the USA has its arsenal trained on China, which in turn threatens the USA and its ally Japan, and a war seems dangerously possible.

The Multiple Threats from Climate Change

Hanging over many of the identified threats to stability identified here, global climate change being the existential crisis is arguably the biggest threat of all. The threat posed by temperature and sea level rises and the science underpinning these predictions have been well understood for many decades, and multiple international conferences have been held to explore these issues and their implications, yet remarkable little real action has been taken, and as a result there now seems little chance that temperature rises will be kept under 1.5°, a target that was agreed at the Paris climate summit in 2015. Once again, the shortcomings of the system of global governance have been made crystal clear.

Given the scale and severity of the problem, it is not surprising that the lack of action has generated so much anger. In the developed countries anger is directed against governments for their lack of resolute action and against energy companies for a perceived lack of honesty about the impacts of their products. In the Global South there is a strong sense that the climate crisis is the direct result of the processes by which the developed countries became rich, but the Global South will feel the most severe impacts of this crisis not of their making. Indeed they are already experiencing the devastating droughts, hurricanes and floods that will only become even more damaging. There has been an expectation that financial assistance will be given in the form of increased aid to fund adaptation and amelioration measures, but such help has fallen far short of these demands. A particular case in point relates to the impact of climate change on migration out of the Global South. People have been seeking better lives in the developed countries for many decades, but climate change will magnify these processes. It is expected, for example, that significant parts of Africa will soon become uninhabitable, incapable of growing the food necessary to support life, giving rise to migration flows of biblical proportions as displaced people seek to find a place where they can survive. Such movements are already underway, of course, as is regularly seen on televisions pictures of boats floundering in the Mediterranean. Many leave their homes to escape poverty, repressive regimes, civil wars and natural disasters, but climate change will fuel massive increases in these desperate flights (Asserate, 2018). In the Global North there is now a strong backlash against further immigration, making the future situation potentially explosive. Climate change will also destabilise global security in a variety of ways. Conflicts over scarce resources, notably water, seem certain to intensify especially in areas where water has always been in short supply. As populations increase, urban centres expand and cash crops are increasingly grown at the expense of basic foodstuffs, conflicts over water will certainly intensify, now magnified by climate change.

Prospects for Improved Global Governance

Given the size, seriousness and complexity of the problems outlined above, it is difficult to envisage a path to a more peaceful, prosperous and equitable future. Inequality at all levels, within communities and nations, within regions and at the global level, is not only increasing dramatically but is made ever more intense by biases in most of the policy reforms that have been introduced in recent years. Under the dominant neoliberal regime, benefits from new initiatives regularly flow overwhelmingly to the top 1% of the population. In the USA, for example, real wages and living standards for the vast majority of the nation have not improved since the 1960s, while a few have become unbelievably rich, creating an economic, social and political environment that is unstable and dangerously polarised. At a global level, the dominant logic is oriented towards the security of a few people living in powerful countries, and the promise of the SDGs to leave no one behind is being relegated to the background. At the same time, the system of global governance known since the end of the Second World War – however imperfect it was – is now in retreat. The multiple factors that are contributing to a new and complex set of interacting crises, or polycrisis, have already been outlined, and it is clear that there is a need to rethink the whole concept of governance in this new, challenging and fundamentally dangerous world. This is no small task, but in the final part of this chapter some thoughts on possible ways forward will be articulated.

So far, each of the major strands that make up the polycrisis has been explored separately, but an important next step is to explore relationships and feedback loops that link together these individual elements. Furthermore, there is also a need to think more clearly about the various spatial scales at which each element of the crisis is operating and try to understand the interaction between these scales. Domestic politics and international relations have always interacted, of course, but in an era of hyper-globalisation the two are now inextricably linked. Similarly, issues of development in the Global South need to be analysed in relation to the changing dynamics of the industrialised world, something that has not always been the case in the past. In such an analysis there is a need to recognise the growing importance of geopolitics and geoeconomics. Geopolitics has a long and complex history, going back at least to the publication by Sir Halford Mackinder of his essay on 'The Geographical Pivot of History', which introduced the concept of the 'Heartland' (Mackinder, 1904). These ideas were taken up enthusiastically by Adolf Hitler and have often been seen as the basis for his obsession with invading the Soviet Union. As a result, the entire field of geopolitics became tainted and pushed aside, but since then there has been dramatic revolution and geopolitics is now a dynamic and rapidly expanding sub-discipline. This is perhaps not surprising given the evidence all around us of competing power blocs and blatant attempts to control territories. Global governance then becomes an exercise in managing geopolitics, an attempt to deal with the collisions now taking place between different national interests, ideologies and aspirations.

Where to begin, then, in dealing with this whirling mass of competing interests and crisis piled upon crisis? An essential first step, as has been argued in the previous chapter, is to ensure that neoliberalism, already seen by many as being in its death-throes, is finally banished as a ruling paradigm. As Bradford DeLong (2022) has argued, neoliberalism has failed to provide the prosperity and 'the good life' that people throughout the world have craved, and indeed have been promised. He believes that neoliberalism can already be described as a failed and discredited project, and therefore that challenge is to design a new economic and political philosophy. However, what comes next will inevitably be influenced by what came earlier and how people have reacted to these failed paradigms. Paolo Gerbaudo (2021) has asserted that the impact of neoliberalism, and the stark levels of inequality that it has created, has caused people to recoil in horror from the world that has been created, and one aspect of this recoil has been the rise of right-wing populism. On the left, by contrast, there has been widespread support for what he describes as a 'vapid cosmopolitanism' that has always helped to sustain neoliberalism and undermine social democracy. While all of this has been playing out, societies were also hit by the multiple impacts of the Covid pandemic and by the mounting evidence of climate change. Some of the impacts of these mounting crises have been undeniably negative, but there may also be some hopeful signs, and in particular the revival of belief in the indispensable roles that may be played by the state.

As it was noted earlier, during the emerging dangers exposed by the GFC, a complete meltdown in the global financial system was only everted by the decisive intervention of the US government, which pumped massive amounts of liquidity into the ailing banks, not only in the USA but also in Europe. Similarly, during the pandemic governments tried to keep citizens safe by organising lockdowns and the distribution of newly developed vaccines. These responses were not always perfect, and they have attracted much criticism (for example, Green, 2021), but there seems little doubt that the involvement of governments was essential, but critical analysis of successes and failures of these interventions is equally vital in considering the current polycrisis.

The initial focus needs to be on the roles of the individual nation states that make up the system of global governance. Under neoliberalism the aim was to strictly limit the size and influence of the state, allowing market forces to determine the allocation of resources. In such *market states* governments were charged with maintaining the rule of law, protecting private property rights and providing some key services in areas such as education and health, but the catch cry was that wherever possible the state should get out of the way. A key indicator of the fall of neoliberalism is that only a minority of citizens now appear to hold this view – the need to protect citizens from terrorism, pandemics and financial chaos have ensured that. Neoliberalism also promoted the idea of looking outwards to the wider world, an increasingly integrated world of trade, investment flows and information exchange. Now there is more interest in looking inwards, promoting nationalism, creating incentives for national development and the generation of local jobs and above all keeping citizens protected – what Gerbaudo (2021) has called *social protectivism*.

In a deeply uncertain and dangerous world it is far from clear that traditional forms of parliamentary democracy are best able to deliver such solace to anxious citizens. The leading democracies all face serious challenges, and not least the USA, often seen as the leading democracy, and India, usually called the world's largest democracy. In an uncertain world the promise of certainty and safety offered by some charismatic authoritarian rulers may be more enticing. In China an unspoken social contract seems to have been agreed: democratic freedoms have been forgone in return for rapid increases in incomes and a more general sense of security. Nationalism is also an attractive force here, and Xi Jinping has certainly stressed his role in building a powerful and proud nation. China's economy is now experiencing some difficulties and how these are resolved, if indeed they can be, will be crucial in determining the future of authoritarian rule in China, and in maintaining the attractiveness of the China model in the Global South.

In an era that is increasingly defined by warfare and the threat of war, the relationships between the state and warfare are increasingly important.

One author who has made a particularly important contribution in this area is Philip Bobbitt. In an earlier book (Bobbitt, 2002) he argued that war was at the centre of the development of the modern state: the treaties that ended each key conflict essentially determined the nature, power and reach of the state. However, the processes of globalisation that were unleashed by neoliberalism also created new threats to the state and to international order. Terrorism became a global phenomenon, one that was able to use new forms of communication and means of propaganda against the state, and in some cases challenge its very existence and legitimacy: is Islamic State really a state, he asks, and is the war on terror really a war (Bobbitt, 2008)?

If the state is seen as essential force for future wellbeing, but is increasingly concerned with national issues relating to welfare and protection of its citizens, what are the implications for the international order and for the future of global governance? Mark Duffield (2001) argued that issues of global development are increasingly being merged with issues of security through the rise of terrorism and the incidence of new forms of war. Conflict resolution and social reconstruction are therefore central concerns in the dialogue about future forms of development, and in the process the very nature of development has been transformed. Thus, building on Duffield's analysis it can be argued that most current problems derive from a malaise of development: the nature and existence of underdevelopment and poverty are the real basis of instability. This is not a new finding, nor is the search for a more inclusive and effective form of development a new endeavour, but the search now has even more urgency.

Conclusion

As it was noted earlier, the liberal global order is under great pressure, and given the multiple crises now besetting the world is being asked to do even more. A key question here is whether there is an alternative to this liberal order. For all its faults the current system still offers the best hope for a better and more stable world, but clearly some fundamental reforms are needed. These views emerge for several reasons. The world is characterised by competition and hostility, but even recognising the intensity of the rivalry between the USA and China, and the new Cold War that it has generated, does not really encompass the true distribution of power in the current environment. A reformed liberal global order must inevitably be based on compromise and the building of consensus, which will be a dauntingly difficult task, but to have any hope of success it must be based on the recognition of a multi-polar world, one in which the Global South also has an important stake. Some coalitions of nations can be helpful here in building consensus: for example, the BRICS include some influential players from the South, as does the G20. Some key international intuitions such as the World Bank and the IMF can be important, but only if substantially reformed. The global financial system as currently constituted inevitably leads to increased levels of inequality and is prone to frequent bouts of instability and chaos. New global pandemics are bound to occur, and the Covid crisis since 2019 has demonstrated that current systems are ill-prepared to deal with such outbreaks and the serious economic disruptions that result. The climate crisis shows that even when there is widespread acceptance of the scientific evidence, agreement on a decisive agenda for action is extremely difficult to achieve. Many of these key issues were the focus of meeting in Paris in June 2023 to discuss how some essential reforms might be funded, and the inability to reach any real form of agreement demonstrated just how difficult it will be to reach consensus, yet it is worthwhile to keep on trying. How to move forward in this multipolar and intensively competitive world is taken up in the next chapters, which deal with the geopolitics of aid, and indeed of the entire development agenda.

References

Adrian, T., & Song, S. H. (2009). *Liquidity and Leverage*. Staff Report No. 328, New York: Federal Reserve Bank of New York.

Allison, G. (2017). *Destined for War: Can America and China Escape Thucydides's Trap?* Boston, MA: Houghton Mifflin.

Asserate, A. W. (2018). *African Exodus: Migration and the Future of Europe*. London: Haus Publishing.

Bobbitt, P. (2002). *The Shield of Achilles*. London: Allen Lane.

Bobbitt, P. (2008). *Terror and Consent: The Wars for the Twenty-First Century*. London: Allen Lane.

Borio, C., James, H., & Song, S. H. (2014). *The International Monetary and Financial System: A Capital Account Historical Perspective*. Basel: Bank of International Settlements, Working Paper No. 457.

Bruno, V., & Song, S. H. (2013). *Capital Flows, Cross Border Banking & Global Liquidity*. Cambridge, MA: National Bureau of Economic Research, Working Paper 19038.

Christophers, B. (2012). Anaemic geographies of financialisation. *New Political Economy*, *17*(3), 271–291.

Christophers, B. (2014). Geographies of Finance I: Historical geographies of the Crisis-Ridden present. *Progress in Human Geography*, *38*(2), 285–293.

Christophers, B. (2015). Geographies of Finance II: Crisis, space & political-economic transformation. *Progress in Human Geography*, *39*(2), 205–213.

Christopherson, S., Martin, R., & Pollard, J. (2013). Financialisation: Roots and repercussions. *Cambridge Journal of Regions, Economy & Society*, *6*, 351–357.

Das, S. (2011). *Extreme Money: The Masters of the Universe and the Cult of Risk*. London: Penguin Books.

DeLong, J. B. (2022). *Slouching Towards Utopia: An Economic History of the Twentieth Century*. New York: Basic Books.

Duffield, M. (2001). *Global Governance and the New Wars: The Merging of Development and Security*. London: Zed Books.

Figes, O. (2022). *The Story of Russia.* London: Bloomsbury.

Gerbaudo, P. (2021). *The Great Recoil: Politics After Populism and Pandemic.* New York: Verso.

Gray, J. (1998). *False Dawn: The Delusions of Global Capitalism.* London: Granta Books.

Green, T. (2021). *The Covid Consensus: The New Politics of Global Inequality.* London: Hurst.

Lapavitsas, C. (2013). *Profiting Without Producing: How Finance Exploits Us All.* New York: Verso.

LeGrand, T. (2022) Politics of Being: Wisdom and Science for a New Development Paradigm, Ocean of Wisdom Press.

Lloyd, P., & Blakemore, M. (2023). Coping in Times of Polycrisis: The Truss Debacle in the Wider Context. Peter Lloyd & Associates. https://www.peter-lloyd.co.uk/papers-and-blogs/

Lo, B. (2023). *The Ukraine Effect: Demise or Rebirth of the Global Order.* Sydney: Lowy Institute.

Mackinder, H. (1904). The geographical pivot of history. *The Geographical Journal, 23*(4), 421–437.

McGregor, R. (2017). *Asia's Reckoning: The Struggle for Global Dominance.* London: Allen Lane.

Roberts, A., & Lamp, N. (2021). *Six Faces of Globalisation: Who Wins, Who Loses, and Why it Matters.* Cambridge, MA: Harvard University Press.

Strange, S. (1986). *Casino Capitalism.* Oxford: Basil Blackwell.

Strange, S. (1997). *Mad Money.* Manchester: Manchester University Press.

Thompson, H. (2022). *Disorder: Hard Times in the 21st Century.* Oxford: Oxford University Press.

Tooze, A. (2018). *Crashed: How a Decade of Financial Crises Changed the World.* London: Allen Lane.

Tooze, A. (2021). *Shutdown: How Covid Shook the World's Economy.* London: Allen Lane.

4 A Critique of Contemporary Foreign Aid

Introduction

Foreign aid within a context of global development is subject to a wide array of forces. The power of the donor is central in a system that is framed around a donor-recipient relationship. Much of the discourse in international development tends towards binary frames of reference – developed/developing, OCED/non-OECD, Western or Northern versus the Global South, traditional versus non-traditional donors, bilateral or multilateral aid. These dichotomies tend to hide nuances that are essential in assessing potential future economic, social and environmental pathways. As noted in Chapter 1, aid is only one part of the complex set of conditions that seek 'good' change; whether this be economic growth, driven by trade, foreign direct investment, domestic and global policy, remittances, social investments, private enterprise and the kind of social and government interventions that frame society are both part of and beyond aid discourse and practice. Relations between and among states are also central, through global governance, conflict and military encounters, financial arrangements and of course the role of global corporations, the private sector and even philanthropic organisations. The debate on international development and aid therefore is both constrained by and contributes to broader global political, economic and social conditions.

There is little dispute around addressing poverty, or basic needs, or responding to crises, yet there is little agreement on what development is or how it can be achieved. International development is inherently a political project, an economic endeavour and/or a social imperative. Throughout the latter half of the 20th century and into the 21st century it is increasingly and critically an ecological project. Foreign aid is thus subject to shifting economic, political and social paradigms, and the focus (or lack therefore) on ecological considerations, whereby the power of the donors in determining the mode and locus of aid and the conditions that govern beneficiaries is indisputable. Moving on from the previous chapters it is clear that the locus of traditional donors (both bilateral and multilateral) in the Global North ensures alignment with the neoliberal aspirations of the power holders of the Global North, key influencers of traditional aid architecture.

DOI: 10.4324/9781003409946-4

Aid is subject to the self-interest of donors and is increasingly linked to the geopolitical forces of great power ambitions of donors. China has been subject to intense scrutiny over its political and economic aspirations embedded in the Belt and Road Initiative (BRI). Russia's role in the world order is writ large and magnified by its invasion of the Ukraine. The USA is caught in a maelstrom of domestic political events that are shaping the storyline not only of foreign aid but also of shifting US leadership globally. The liberal international order, framing traditional foreign aid discourse and practice, is under stress from both internal and external sources. Beyond the global political economic context, there is a corresponding geographical shift in development discourse. This shift is, in simplistic terms, towards an increasing notion of development framed around power and reconsiders the validity of development as an endeavour of the Global North expanding a vision of modernity, driven by globalised, market-based neoliberal model that can be transposed to the Global South. The reversal of development gains adds a level of complexity to the debate, as this global context of growth and development has been challenged by inequality, climate and environmental concerns, and in the contemporary context by the polycrisis. Aid, in terms of how it is conceptualised, how much, where and how it is allocated, gives some shape to understanding these forces, a topic that is analysed in depth in Chapter 5.

This chapter reviews dominant constructions of aid and development over time, followed by determination of aid flows and development trends in the contemporary context, against the foreground of the prominent reversal of development gains and the links to contemporary crises. The chapter reflects on evolving role of power and political economy of aid distribution, and the rise of non-traditional actors, decolonising discourses and calls for power shifts from the Global South. Within this complex contested space, the chapter turns to an assessment of the impact of Covid and a post-Covid development context, the war in Ukraine and climate emergency, to consider the potential impacts on core aspects of the Sustainable Development Goals (SDGs), poverty, the food, economic and other forms of humanitarian crises. The chapter concludes by demonstrating that foreign aid and development is complex, contested, geostrategic, political and economic space, subject to extensive focus of the self-interest of the Global North, leaving it open to potential abduction for nefarious purposes.

International Development and Foreign Aid

Foreign aid in its post-war identity, framed within an architecture of large western-led multilateral development and finance institutions, donor governments, non-government and civil society-based actors and increasingly philanthropic and private sector players, has always been a contested project, ideologically, theoretically and practically. A paradigm of international development, that of a differentiation between a Global North and South, developed versus developing, rich versus poor and a resulting intentional effort to 'develop' those who are underdeveloped, has persisted across the intervening nearly eight decades. There have been fundamental, seismic shifts in this time, including in global power and politics and in economic ideology which, as Chapter 2 denotes, despite significant and ongoing critique, currently feels like circling the eternal cul-de-sac of neoliberalism. Shifts from an east/west to north/south framing of technological, social, political and economic superiority, and discourses on the securitisation of aid, of the effectiveness of aid, the need for good governance, the coloniality or even futility of aid, have lined a highway that has not led to western style development in most cases. The materialisation of the negative impacts of a model of development contingent on modernised 'western' vision of development increasingly challenges the economic growth mindset of human wellbeing. Planetary boundaries (Steffan et al., 2015) are becoming centralised in discourse, if not institutional change. The SDGs underpinning the development policy of traditional development space since 2015 are currently moving further out of reach.

Non-traditional donors and actors are increasingly embroiled in economic development, global governance and discourse. Most recent shifts identify the coloniality of the entrenched aid system, and a need, if not necessarily a trend, to 'shift the power'[1] (Martins, 2021). The emergence of demand-driven systems change draws heavily on localisation discourses emerging from within the humanitarian space (Kelly et al., forthcoming). These 'politics' of aid and development, in particular the vested interests of donors, recipients and the institutions and sectors that frame this relationship, are underpinned by inequalities of power and agency, issues that have imbued development theorising for decades (Mawdsley et al., 2014).

Knutsson (2009: 2), in recognising development as an 'essentially contested concept', argues that any conceptualisation of development is related to societal aims and how society understands and attempts to intervene in problems. A key issue, of course, is that this changes over time, and the current context of crises appears, in current consideration (although history may well tell a different tale), a point of significant flux. At a meta-theoretical level paradigmatic shifts can be found, for example, between and within Monetarist orthodox and Marxist heterodox economics (see Dow, 2011), and paradigms of power relationships within and between donors, and recipients (cf. Rist, 2003; Hettne, 2010; Nederveen Pieterse, 2010; Peet & Hartwick, 2015; Carmody, 2019).

Given that mainstream development discourse (discursive, normative and institutional) is framed within the capitalist economy, and since the 1980s within a neoliberal capitalist development sphere, the interlinkages between economic ideology and political/power theories become central in considering the many paradoxes of capitalism, in particular uneven development.

There are two distinct crises associated with global capitalism: the first is the simultaneous creation of wealth and poverty, and the second is the ecological crisis. Samir Amins (1974) highlighted the relevance of the polarising nature of global capitalism, in the context of development, although notably his later work went beyond core periphery models, arguing for thinking critically about global structures that reproduce Eurocentric prejudice and thus imperialist and racist foundations of capitalist system (Ndlovu-Gatsheni, 2021). Capitalism is indeed the epitome of paradox, not only demonstrating a tendency towards crisis, change and instability but also having an ability to stabilise institutions, rules and norms. Inequality and planetary ecological crisis, predominantly the impact of a changing climate, are two consequential outcomes of this. Piketty (2020) argues a clear link between colonial domination and appropriation, the rise of a private ownership society and the extreme and rising inequality of the present (building on his 2014 exposition on the embeddedness of inequity in the current capitalist system).

The unevenness (Harvey, 2006) of modernistic, capitalist development requires and is subject to political economy analysis. A political economy of aid must, as Büscher[2] (2019) argues, not only consider the 'extreme volatility in contemporary political economic fortunes across and between spaces of the world economy' (Harvey, 2006: 71, cited by Büscher, 2019: 485), but must also consider theorisations of development. To deeply engage in political economy of development therefore also must position debates in historical and geographical context. Foreign aid as an end in itself, the fulfilment of an obligation of rich countries to those in need, is one end of a spectrum of rationale for the giving of money under the banner of foreign aid. Towards the other end of this spectrum is the self-interests of donors. Within this narrative, global cooperation for development, equality, social justice, stability and environmental sustainability frames global governance models that emerged from the post-World War II moment. Woods (2005: 394) reflected on challenges to foreign aid in the post-9/11 scenario, highlighting that aid has always been subject to geostrategic interests. During the Cold War aid was governed by geostrategic goals and primarily as a product of ideological differences between the USA and the then USSR.

Politically and economically development aid in its current form emerged from the interests of the USA and Allies in the post-World War II context, with the establishment of the Bretton Woods institutions, providing a central point for an emerging aid and development architecture which persists today, comprising the World Bank and IMF, other International Financial Institutions (ADB, AfDB, etc.), the United Nations and associated agencies, Non-Government Organisations which gained significant prominence, with an 'explosion' (Brass et al., 2018: 136) in numbers of development NGOs from the 1980s, donors, government and private sector all key stakeholders, albeit with shifting levels of engagement and power. Without providing an in-depth history of foreign aid (ably provided by Rist, 2002) it is clear that development aid in its post-World War II inception is a contested project, ideologically, theoretically and practically. A paradigm of international development, that of a differentiation between a Global North and South, a developed versus developing and a resulting intentional effort to 'develop' those who are underdeveloped has persisted across the intervening nearly eight decades.

Knutsson (2009: 2), in recognising development as an 'essentially contested concept', argues that any conceptualisation of development is related to societal aims and how society understands and attempts to intervene in problems. A key issue of course is that this changes over time. Hettne (2009) argues that 'various schools of development thinking should be contextualized historically, rather than understood as a cumulative evolution of ideas towards a universal development theory' (p. 9). Development nevertheless has been predominantly associated with a post-World War II development architecture, as outlined above.

Multilateralism sits at the heart of global cooperation. Approaching the 80th anniversary of the Bretton Woods conference (1944) there is little change to the structures that emerged, at the World Bank and the International Monetary Fund (IMF), despite a number of ideological changes. The United Nations emerged in 1945, with a similar mandate – 'international peace and security…humanitarian assistance to those in need, protect human rights, and uphold international law' (UN.org). Its mandate has expanded to include many aspects of development policy and practice, setting development goals, currently the SDGs, and increasingly centring climate action. The mantra of the United Nations is 'One place where the world's nations can gather together, discuss common problems and find shared solutions' (www.un.org/about-us). The representation of the majority world within the UN system has been consistently subject also to critique. However, the World Economic Forum (2022) highlighted multilateralism (and state) collapse as one of the critical threats over the next five to ten years.

The liberal international order within traditional foreign aid discourse and practice is under stress from both internal and external sources. Thus, the existing Western hegemonic neoliberal development aid paradigm is being challenged from within and without. From within, challenges come from combinations of economic and political shifts. Inflationary pressures, costs of living crises and the rather gloomy outlook for the global economy are challenging domestic commitments to aid flows in donor countries, although notably the UK is only one of the 'big five' donors to reduce aid flows in response to economic and political pressures. Politicly, antagonistic sentiments towards globalisation, nationalistic discourses (America First) drive right-wing populist discourses that saw commitments to multilateralism and aid flows challenges by Trumpist policies in the USA. As Regilme (2022) concluded, despite Trump's failure to provide a coherent and credible discourse either with regard to addressing the growing influence of China as a donor or with regard to anti-globalisation and nationalistic discourse, there was reputational damage to the USA in terms of its dominant role in global governance. The Biden administration acted quickly to reinstate a commitment to global governance and aid. Both go some way to restoring reputational damage, but also flag some precarity of global aid flows. Therefore, internal threats relate primarily to the self-interest of donors, within a context of crisis and their continued commitment to the provision of aid.

External threats relate most strongly to non-traditional actors in aid and development and the implications not only of the geostrategic competition for hearts and minds that aid in part engenders, but also in the impact of non-traditional aid distributions and modalities. Challenges to the traditional aid framing are of course subject to shifting world global power poles, the no longer new impact of 'non-traditional' donors, through both south-south and triangular cooperation. The role of China's Belt and Road Initiative is of significance in terms of global infrastructure investment, and the slowdown of the Chinese economy of major concern. However, the rise of philanthropic spending within an aid context is equally significant across health and agriculture with reference to the ideology of the Gates Foundation. The implications of where funding or investment comes from are vital in considering political and economic impact. This relates much more broadly than just implications for 'recipient' country governance through conditionalities, but fundamental shifts in power, of nation states, or regions, and of corporations and philanthropic entities, that are impacting directly and explicitly on, for example, the food and health systems. To delve further into these complexities the following section turns to aid flows, both traditional and non-traditional.

Dominant Constructions of Aid Over Time

Challenges to international development, in its dominant guise of institutions led by the Global North, with all the associated economic and political implications of this relationship have never been so strident, with the limitations of 'western' development models more evident. Within this, there is an ever-evolving range of theories on how change happens, and thus whether and how intentional rather than immanent development prevails. Dominant constructions of aid over time fall broadly, if somewhat simplistically, into two camps: conventional development theorisation and a counterhegemonic theoretical lens. A conventional capitalist, neoliberal development theorisation is based on western hegemonic economic discourse, framed solidly within modernisation, capitalism, and related liberal economic order.

Conventional Theorisation of Development Aid

The notion of a need for a 'modern' versus less modern or traditional society, driven by economic growth, underpins much of the conventional development theorisation. Two major paths to modernisation in the post-war era were capitalism and Marxism. Capitalist discourse, drawing in part on Rostov's (1959) stages of development, and driven by the USA, dominated development from the 1950s onwards, being in essence an extension of the Marshall plan, as outlined previously. It was in essence a monolithic, state-centric, one-way and top-down approach based on democratic and secular political structures. In this vision, economic development, political change and cultural change go together (Rostov, 1959; Escobar, 1995; Chirot & Hall, 1982).

A capitalist neoliberal development paradigm, based on mainstream economic discourse survived, although critiqued, almost unscathed until the GFC. Even in the current times, post-Washington consensus, or neo-structuralist post-neoliberalism (Murray & Overton, 2011), the dominance of a neoliberal agenda is evident across most aspects of foreign aid, even while the pillars of neoliberalism are crumbling under its failings. Despite development theories focused on the failings of the modernisation/capitalist vision of development, the shift, economically, to capitalist neoliberal development did nothing to counter western dominance globally, and in particular the US- and UK-led political economy model. Neoliberal development theory is both a modification of and an expansion of modernisation, shifting away from structuralist policies of the 1950s. Arguably the current economic context of post-Washington consensus, or more broadly, post-neoliberal (in the broader sense, rather than in Latin American conceptualisation) retains the basic premise of neoliberalism, casting underdevelopment as a problem of mismanagement (Pieterse, 2010). Critiques of neoliberal development models spawned a 'Post-Washington Consensus' model of development that refocused on the role of the state in regulating markets, under the banner of 'good governance'. Murray and Overton (2011) argue for mixed populist calls for human rights and democracy with reform of governments to ensure transparency and accountability. They further argue that the neo-structuralist model of post-neoliberal development embedded in the 2000s was acceptable, in that it trod a fine line between society and the market, thus rendering it acceptable to centre left politics, remaining non-threatening to capitalist elite, with some promise of benefits to the marginalised.

It was argued in Chapter 2 that a further factor in favour of neoliberalism, in diverse guises, is the lack of alternatives. Neoliberalism continues in altered forms adapting and morphing, due to no clear alternative. Even in the current times the dominance of a neoliberal agenda is evident across most aspects of foreign aid, even while the pillars of neoliberalism are crumbling under its failings. However, the notion that there is no alternative (as Margaret Thatcher frequently claimed with regard to economic liberalism) is challenged by counter hegemonic discourse.

Counter Hegemonic Theoretical Lens

There has been no shortage of alterative conceptualisations of how society can change. From early critiques based on Marxist understandings around the organisation of capital and labour, perhaps the defining aspects of counter-hegemonic theoretical positions are a conceptualisation of society based not around economic growth and organisation, but more so about the interrelation-ships between the past and the present (decolonial and post-colonial theories), about power and control within and between nations (World Systems Theory (WST), Dependency Theory)), about social goals, outside of monetary or eco-nomic visions of modernity (post-development), and most significantly given the dominant 'Western' politic al and economic values, and ideologies, the fo-cus on non-western values, ideologies, paradigms and knowledge's. This later critique goes to the core of international development and foreign aid, calling to account the very notion of externally driven 'development'. The idea of a north south or western/non-western binary is questioned, with the spectre of power discourse embedded in an idea of the lesser 'third world' (Horner, 2020). Said's (1978) analysis of a presumption of western superiority as a po-litical instrument of domination has resonated through resulting development discourse. Naylor (2011) argues that international development is best con-ceptualised through underlying structural inequalities or relations of power that are maintained and reconstituted through a politics of pity, which relies upon and perpetuates the very poverty and inequality international develop-ment claims to eradicate. Recent iterations of development from a theoretical and critical perspective incorporate critical development theory that moved beyond the somewhat conceptual debate of the post-development work of Sachs (1992), Said (1978) and Escobar (1995), for example, that framed the whole development enterprise as illusion requiring a more power-sensitive theory of change.

Critical Development Studies (CDS) is the more recent field of enquiry and debate, which takes a broader and evolving counter hegemonic stance, combining political economy with social ecology. Bowles and Veltmeyer (2021) identify four characteristics of CDS, intended as an attempt to distin-guish CDS from mainstream development rather than as a defining moment. These indicative and non-exclusive characteristics are first a focus on the underlying impact of the crisis of capitalism as a fundamental contradiction to development. The second characteristic is a critical lens on development as a way of analysing the notion of a better life, while challenging prevail-ing orthodoxies. Third is the articulation and implementation of resistance to capitalism at the periphery of the world capitalism system (such as is seen in Bolivia in Buen Vivir for example in van Norren (2020). The articulation and practice of resistance to the advance of capitalism are not new, as noted in WST, Dependency theory and Marxist critiques. The fourth characteristic is the capacity to conceive of underdevelopment or peripheral capitalist development in some contexts, and post-capitalist or alternative developments in others depending on the unevenness of development, and its experience in different parts of the periphery (Bowles & Veltmeyer, 2021). Running through and alongside CDS are paradigms of coloniality/modernity, feminist discourses and rapidly evolving discourses around race and racism, power and more than human modalities of development. The framing of the relationship between the Global North and South, in a rapidly evolving context of shifting geopolitics, is not only in shifting poles of power, and great power ambitions of the USA, China and recently Russia, but also in the demands for power sharing and recognition from the Global South. These discourses and demands draw on decades of critique of the disproportionate control of political and economic global institutions that are subject to much of this counter-hegemonic discourse.

As becomes clear, development as conceptualised as a binary between developed and developing, modern and traditional, has less and less relevance in an era of 'global development'. Concerns of inequality, climate emergency and other planetary boundaries, as well as public health issues are global in nature, and the conceptual underpinnings of a global development industry premised on a 'western' vision of a developed nation, in a contemporary context where so called developed nations are no longer the bastion of modernity, an imagined state of development. It further demonstrates that despite 70 plus years of significant critique, from diverse and counterhegemonic standpoints, international development, as represented through its main proponents, the World Bank and IMF, has failed to shift in any significant way from the hegemonic economic and political paradigms of the USA and her allies in the development endeavour. Although this is a simplification of 75 years of development discourse, white western economic paradigms have driven an aid system that remains powerful. There is a clear failure of the New International Economic Order, the lack of impact of dependency theorists, post-development theorists, Marxist critiques, feminist critiques, critical development theory and the decolonial scholars to impact meaningfully, to date, on a free-market-driven, western-led international aid and development system. This amply demonstrates that these are indeed counter-hegemonic discourses and thus can be safely either ignored or 'mainstreamed' in a way that renders any response to critique unthreatening to the status quo, in terms of global power relations and the position of the 'West'. At the moment there is no new paradigm emerging, a vastly concerning thought, when positioned against the context of a polycrisis. Although globally and within development thinking we are currently clearly in a phase of transition, there is no clear paradigmatic alternative to the existing, thus we are in essence on a transition to nowhere. The above discourse considers aid within a lens of how a better society may be achieved, and as is eminently clear, there is little agreement!

There is value in further positioning aid discourse within competing goals of creating a better society, and in terms of the self-interest of the donor. Aid is by its very nature limited and therefore decisions must be made, not only on how to spend it, and on what, but how much aid is allocated, and where, and through which mechanisms to spend it.

Aid Flows and Development Trends

Resource flows to non-OECD countries comprise three major forms. Figure 4.1 shows the relative volume and growth in FDI, remittances and aid, using Official Development Assistance (ODA) as a measure, to Least Developed Countries (LDCs). LDCs are a good case study of relative flows, given their status, as defined by the UN, as low-income countries with severe structural impediments to sustainable development, and vulnerable to economic and environmental shocks. They comprise 46 countries at the current time.[3] As can be seen below ODA has comprised the greatest resources flows to LDCs. However, there has been a steady increase in remittances, which is now on a par with ODA. FDI in this context is not a stable source of finance, subject to significant fluctuations over the previous decade. With regard to FDI, investment to low- and middle-income countries is volatile with 2020 FDI of 536.1 billion (USD), 2021 FDI of 761.8 billion (USD) and 2022 figures of 182.73 billion (USD). Remittances are significant globally.

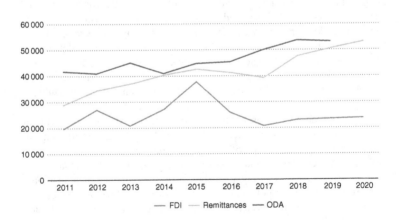

Figure 4.1 LDCs: FDI, ODA and Remittances 2011–2020.

Source: OECD (2023), FDI flows (indicator). doi: 10.1787/99f6e393-en (Accessed on 19 June 2023).

IFAD notes that around one billion people worldwide depend on remittances, with an estimated 200 million migrant workers a year sending money home (IFAD, 2023). World Bank data show that remittances received in LDCs totalled US$59 billion in 2022. Low-income countries received 13 billon, but low- and middle-income countries combined received US$592 billion (World Bank – https://data.worldbank.org/indicator/BX.TRF.PWKR.CD.DT)

The context within which aid flows are committed and disbursed is a rapidly evolving environment. Covid-19 required increased requirement for aid, in many cases in tightening donor spaces for commitments, and the emergence of the Ukraine context frames a range of compounding and cascading crises.

ODA is resource flows to countries and territories on the Development Assistance Committee of the OECD list of ODA recipients:

1 'Provided by official agencies, including state and local governments, or by their executive agencies; and
2 Concessional (i.e. grants and soft loans) and administered with the promotion of the economic development and welfare of developing countries as the main objective'.

ODA measures donor efforts, including grants and grant equivalent of concessional loans. ODA as a defined measure evolved from the work of the Development Assistance Committee of the newly minted OECD in 1961. The DAC emerged as a forum for consultations of aid donors. The aim of the DAC, agreed through the 'Common Aid Effort', was to increase the flow of resources to less developed countries, through improved terms and conditions associated with aid, and therefore its effectiveness. In the early 1960s the US provided more than 40% of ODA, and the UK and France, around one-third (OECD, 2006).

Official Development Assistance totalled USD $204 billion in 2022, an all-time high and the fourth consecutive year that ODA reached new heights (OECD, 2023). This was up from US$185.9 billion in 2021 (OECD, 2023a), equating to 0.33% of GNI, against a long-standing target of 0.7% GNI for donor countries[4] Notably, 70% of ODA comes from just five countries: the USA, Germany, Japan, the UK and France. The overall rise in aid flows would have been 8% higher in real terms had ODA remained stable. Six countries had ODA volume falls, against 23 countries where volumes rose in 2021. The rises were often due to support for Covid-19 responses (Ahmed & Carey, 2022).

Within the overall 2022 ODA budget, just under 11% was humanitarian aid (up 1% from 2021). Five percent of ODA went to Covid-19-related activities (down 45% from 2021), and vaccine donations comprised 0.75%, a 74% reduction from 2021. Debt relief was negligible at US$60 million (0.02%). Gross bilateral ODA comprised 82% grants (18% loans and equity investments). For LDCs, ODA comprises over two-thirds of external finance (not including non-DAC donors) (OECD, 2023). A breakdown of 2022 figures, however, shows that bilateral aid to Africa fell 7.4% year on year. Bilateral aid to LDC also fell by 0.7%. Several aspects of current aid flows are subject to criticisms. The first is what can be seen as inflating aid. Examples include costs of hosting refugees locally (more on this below). The second is in examples such as the offloading of goods as aid. A specific example is found within the 1.53 billion in vaccine doses which are counted as ODA. However, Chadwick (2023) reports that only US$16 million were doses that were specially purchased as aid donation rather than initially for domestic citizen use within the donor country that ended up being excess to demand.

Beyond these high-level figures, there is controversy over where and how aid is counted, which has direct relevance to understanding the above figures. Metrics for determining foreign aid flows have become increasingly complex, not only in how they are measured but more importantly how aid is conceptualised and allocated. As outlined in Chapter 1, ODA increased 218% in real terms between 2000 and 2021 (OECD, 2022). ODA has been, since the 1960s, the standard for measuring resource flows from richer to poorer countries. It is both a highly technical and a highly political concept. The definition of ODA, updated in 2021, and in 2016 with regard to what constitutes ODA, and clarification of eligibility of items in the grey space of support in conflict contexts are highly relevant to understanding implications of the Ukraine war on ODA, and implications for non-Ukraine crises, including worsening metrics around poverty, food security and other humanitarian crises.

The nearly 14% increase in ODA from 2021 to 2022, although a highly positive trend, was primarily due to a significant increase, and accounting for the cost of processing and hosting donors within the borders of the donor country – 'in donor' refugee costs, which accounted for over US$29 billion in 2023 (14.4% of total ODA), up from US$12.8 billion in 2021 (OECD, 2023). War and conflict resulting in significant population displacements increased spending on refugees in countries subject to increased people movements, thus impacting on overall spend internationally. The inclusion of refugee costs in ODA budgets is somewhat inconsistent. Given the dramatic people movements of 2015, the 'European Refugee Crisis', of more than 1 million refugees claiming asylum in Europe (of an estimated 1.5 million in OECD countries), there was significant increase in spending on refugees 'in donor countries'. In the period from 2016 to 2018, the OECD clarified eligibility rules for ODA for Peace and Security as well as 'in donor refugee costs' which is limited to the first year post-arrival of certain domestic costs associated with refugee arrivals.

There are an estimated 108 million forcibly displaced peoples globally, of which 35 million are refugees (UNHCR, 2023). Just over half of them come from three countries: the Syrian Arab republic (6.8 million), Ukraine (5.7 million) and Afghanistan (5.7 million). In regard to numbers of Ukrainian refugees, Poland hosts over 1.5 million, Germany hosts just over 1 million, the Czech Republic just hosts under half a million, and numbers down from there fall to the UK with around 200,000 (Trebesch et al., 2023). Interestingly, though, the UK spent a similar amount to Germany of around 4.5 billion. Germany, however, reported these costs as additional to their planned development budget. None of the G8 funded all their costs of Ukrainian Refugees from within their existing aid budget, except the UK. Further, the UK did not impose any cap on the amount of in-donor refugee costs, resulting in inefficiency, and requiring even further cuts to other parts of the budget.

The UK spent 29% of its total ODA budget on in-donor refugee costs in 2022 (OECD, 2023). This represents a 16% decrease in ODA to non-domestic sources. The UK Independent Commission for Aid Impact (ICAI) review of these costs found that 'the ability of departments to spend an unlimited proportion of the aid budget on the first year costs of asylum seekers and refugees undermines incentives for longer term planning to reduce costs, risking poor value for money' (ICAI, 2023: np). They also found that this issue has negatively impacted on UK aid, as all but essential aid was paused to meet the high (and inefficient) costs of refugees within the UK, resulting in delays and limited capacity for humanitarian response in other context, such as floods in Pakistan and Somalia food crisis (ICAI, 2023). ICAI (2023) noted that the UK spend on supporting refugee and asylum seekers in the UK was double the average of other donors (ICAI, 2023), but the impact was not necessarily as severe. Poland, for example, utilised 65% of its total ODA on in-donor refugee costs, and the Republic of Ireland 51%. Yet both counties realised an increase in ODA *not* including in-donor refugee costs, Poland achieved a 28% increase and Ireland 15%. Hynes and Scott back in 2013 proposed a new ODA measure that explicitly excluded domestic expenditures on in-donor refugees as well as overseas students, and 'development awareness' programmes.

In defining what ODA is, the OECD also defines what it is not. ODA is *not*, according to OECD (2023) definitions, '*Military aid and promotion of donors' security interests*' (np). In the context of Ukraine it is instructive to explore total resource flows from donors, which includes humanitarian, financial and military aid. Total government to government resource flows to Ukraine between January 2022 and January 2023 total an estimated US$143 billion (Trebesch et al., 2023). A further 13 US$ billion flows in from multilateral institutions (World Bank, IMF and others). This includes humanitarian, financial and military aid. However, a quick comparison of total government to government resource flows into the Ukraine of US143 billion versus a total ODA spend globally of 204 billion is instructive. The US is the biggest donor, contributing more than 50% of the resource flows to Ukraine in the period from January 2022 to January 223 (Trebush et al., 2023) and therefore a useful case study to understand in a more nuanced fashion total resource flows.

A review of total US spending to Ukraine compiled by the Kiel Institute for the World Economy shows that between January 2022 and February 2023 the US committed US$78.6 billion. Just 5% of this sum is humanitarian aid. Financial flows comprise 34%. Total military assistance comprised 61% broken down into 24% security assistance (training, equipment weapons, logistics support and so on). About 31% is weapons and equipment from the Défense Department, and a further 6% in the form of grants and loans for weapons and equipment. This military aid is not accountable as ODA, but given that it more than doubles resource flows to this one country it is notable in the context of this discourse. Discussions with regard to the rebuilding of Ukraine are underway. Reconstruction costs are, according to Becker et al. (2022), likely to be in the realm of thousands of billions of dollars.

In a bigger historical picture, aid to Ukraine appears comparatively limited. For example, the US spent many times more per year on the Korea, Vietnam or Iraq wars (measured in percent of GDP). The same is true for Germany during the Gulf War of 1990/1991, where it committed more than three times as much to liberate Kuwait compared to what Germany has bilaterally committed to Ukraine in 2022. In more recent Trebesch et al. (2023) note that European countries mobilised 8 times more for the EU's response to the Covid-19 crisis, under the Next Generation EU (NGEU) recovery programme, and 4 times more resources for Eurozone bailouts (primarily to Portugal, Ireland Greece and Spain) during the Eurozone crisis after 2010 (Trebesch et al., 2023).

The ability of donors to respond to Ukraine for geostrategic purposes is widely noted, although the hype appears slightly more impressive than the actual figures. However, the geostrategic channelling of aid is neither new nor indeed remarkable, as can be seen by a quick perusal of American and German aid as examples.

Aid from the US, or 'USAID from the American People', as the USAID slogan proclaims, is predominantly focused on Africa and the Middle East, with 38.9% of bilateral ODA for Africa and 11.3% to the Middle East. More than 99% of ODA is in the form of grants, and Jordan is the top recipient of US aid flows at 217 million dollars, followed by Afghanistan, Nigeria, Ethiopia, DRC, South Sudan, South Africa, Yemen, Somalia and Syria. US bilateral aid is almost entirely (>99%) in the form of grants. The US is below DAC average (44%) in percentage of funding though the public sector at 30%. Earmarked funding through multilaterals in 2021 was 23% (against a 26% DAC average), and 21% was allocated through NGOs and CSOs (against a DAC average of 17%) (Donor Tracker, 2023).

Aid flows to Jordan are complex. The strategic location of Jordan as US and UK ally in the Middle East is one part of a complex puzzle. Its location bordering Syria, Iraq and Israel (as well as Saudi Arabia) exposes the Hashemite Kingdom of Jordan to demographic and economic shocks due to population movements, hosting hundreds of thousands of refugees, a continuation of Jordan's position as a hotspot for refugees. The political and economic nature of refuges in the region is argued by Kelberer (2017) to provide fertile grounds for effective 'refugee rentierism' by Jordan, in essence using its status of refugee host, and policies as political leverage for gaining international 'rent' or humanitarian and development aid, in a state that in 2022, was defined as upper middle-income state.

Germany, in 2022, was the second largest provider of development cooperation funding, and the only one of the 'big five' to meet the 0.7 GNI target (at 0.74%, 2021). Just under 80% of total German ODA of USD\$ 32 billion in 2021 was bilateral, predominantly implemented by GIZ and KfW agencies, led by the Federal Ministry for Economic Cooperation and Development (BMZ). Germany's top-ten recipients are predominantly middle-income countries (OECD, 2022). Nearly 40% of ODA was allocated to middle-income countries (OECD – DAC, 2022); the 13.4% of Gross Bilateral ODA allocated to LDCs is significantly below the 24.4 % DAC average. Öhm's (2021) consideration of German development cooperation notes that renewed geostrategic global concerns will likely require greater geostrategic focus. This is despite an history of relatively non-partisan aid policy up to recent times. He highlights a reconciliation of Germany's colonial past through reparations to Namibia, as well as the relevance of German focus on forced migration to its recent focus on African continent and Indo-Pacific guidelines. Unsurprisingly, German aid is likely to align at some level with European joint and multilateral approaches.

These cases demonstrate at a high level the gulf between countries use of aid within the geopolitical or geostrategic space. In addition, so called non-traditional donors contribute significant aid flows, impacting both development outcomes and also development policy and discourse.

Non-Traditional Donors

The impact of 'non-traditional' or non-DAC donors has evolved rapidly over the past two decades, from early discussions on Saudi Arabia and the so-called BRICS (Brazil, Russia, India, China and South Africa) (Kragelund, 2010). In 2019 of the total global development flows estimated by the OECD, 14% or an estimated USD\$24 billion dollars were by non-DAC donors, including both reporting and non-reporting non-DAC donors.

The most prominent shift in aid flows is China. Going from an aid-recipient country at the turn of the century to one of the biggest donors within 20 years, the impact of China on aid flows, on the development architecture and on the geopolitical implications for aid, is central to any contemporary discussion on aid. Accurate figures for Chinese foreign aid are complex. Ye (2022) reports that around US\$ 3.1 billion of Chinese foreign aid was disbursed in 2020, primality to countries in Africa. Yet Muggah (2023) calculates that if all development financing was included, Chinese support is much closer to US$85 billion. Regardless of absolute volumes it is clear that Chinese global reach is both extensive and impactful. There has been a significant recent drop in infrastructure lending for Chinese Belt and Road Initiative which many note as stalling somewhat (Lu, 2023).

Critique of the impact of Chinese investment through loans associated with the BRI is emerging, and many are associated with the existing debt crisis that has embroiled many poor countries. Zambia and Sri Lanka have both defaulted on their debts, adding fuel to the critique of Chinese Debt trap diplomacy. However, Hsiang (2023) argues that a neocolonial reading of China's intentions in Zambia is perhaps too convenient, as despite the fact that Zambia has the largest number of Chinese lenders in Africa, this still only compromises 18% of total external debt. Lu (2023) notes the rather haphazard implementation of the BRI lending, with limited oversight or risk analysis, and thus the economic viability of BRI loans was never in focus. Condon (2023) highlights a much more disturbing impact of the debt crisis. He argues that there is a resulting geopolitical instability driven by Chinese reluctance to forgive debt, resulting in a stalemate where other lenders are unwilling to step in or forgive non-Chinese debt. In this stalemate the spectre of further defaults and political upheaval is not inconceivable.

Discussion and Conclusions

What does all of this mean for the existing context of polycrises? This chapter concludes by demonstrating that foreign aid and development is complex, contested, political and economic space, subject to extensive focus of the self-interest of the Global North, leaving it open to potential abduction for nefarious purposes.

International aid and development is centred within a complex political and economic space which is as much ideological as it is philanthropic. The power of traditional or Northern donors in determining a global political economy is in somewhat of a crisis itself. Late stage capitalism and the injuries enacted through neoliberal development models in the Global North and south are clear. Dominant or mainstream development conceptualisations are continuing, but within a shrinking space of influence. Critiques of aid, highlighted in this chapter through a closer exploration of aid flows and trends, demonstrate just how complex development is. ODA is a solid contributor to global development and humanitarian contexts. Yet it is largely insufficient. Donor decisions with regard to not only where to concentrate funds but also on what and the implications of this raise significant questions as to whether development resourcing can address development and humanitarian challenges. As can be seen by what is in essence a comparatively limited response in Ukraine, that has impacted expenditure elsewhere. The commitment of donors to development aid, either through DAC ODA channels directly or for non-traditional donors through their own channels, is clearly and explicitly subject to political considerations, and increasingly geostrategic considerations. These are driven by domestic accountability concerns, as well as international geostrategic concerns. The US remains a major player in global development and humanitarian financing. China has risen to be of similar stature, yet through highly diverse mechanisms and modalities. The 'great power' struggle between the USA and China explicitly drives development discourse and practice, not only ideologically, but with regard to gaining influence and power. However, bilateral relations, regional relations and global concerns influence every donor. The relationship between aid and need is at best unclear and at worst increasingly dissociated from policy and practice. The potential for aid to be increasingly open to abduction for geopolitical and geostrategic purposes is apparent, given the embedded self interest of the donor in existing global aid architectures, both traditional and emerging. The following chapter picks up the geopolitical thread further.

Notes

1 #ShiftThePower emerged from the 2016 https://globalfundcommunityfoundations. org/.
2 Büscher is writing here in critique of Horner and Hulme, 2019 who argue for a reconceptualization from International Development to Global Development.
3 https://www.un.org/development/desa/dpad/least-developed-country-category. html.
4 Met only by Denmark (0.7%), Germany (0.83%), Luxembourg (1.00%), Norway (0.86%) and Sweden (0.90%).

References

Ahmed, Y., & Carey, E. (2022). How Covid-19 and Russia's war of aggression against Ukraine are reshaping official development assistance (ODA). *Development Cooperation Profiles, in OECD (2022)*. https://www.oecd-ilibrary.org/sites/223ac1dd-en/ index.html?itemId=/content/component/0079f636-en&_csp_=2e70060d368b5fc38 b205b10ce2ddda6&itemIGO=oecd&itemContentType=chapter#section-d1e61

Amin, S. (1974). *Accumulation on a World Scale*. Sussex: Harvester Press.

Becker, T., Eichengreen B., Gorodnichenko Y., Guriev S., Johnson S., Mylovanov T., Rogoff K., & Weder di Mauro, B. (2022), *A Blueprint for the Reconstruction of Ukraine*, CEPR Press.

Brass, Jennifer N. & Longhofer, Wesley & Robinson, Rachel S. & Schnable, Allison, 2018. "NGOs and international development: A review of thirty-five years of scholarship," *World Development*, Elsevier, vol. 112(C), pages 136–149.

Büscher, B. (2019). From 'Global' to 'Revolutionary' development. *Development and Change, 50*, 484–494.

Carmody, P. (2019). *Development Theory and Practice in a Changing World*. Abingdon: Routledge.

Chadwick, V. (2023). Ukraine war triggers record aid levels, and fresh criticism for OECD. *Devex*, April 13. https://www.devex.com/news/ukraine-war-triggers-record-aid-levels-and-fresh-criticism-for-oecd-105289#:~:text=The%20Organisation%20for%20Economic%20Co-operation%20and%20Development%20has,bilateral%20support%20to%20Africa%20and%20least-developed%20countries%20decreased

COndon, B. (2023) MAY 26, 2023 China's loans pushing world's poorest countries to brink of collapse, Associate Press, https://leads.ap.org/best-of-the-week/chinas-loans.

Donor Tracker. (2023). *Donor Country Profiles*. https://donortracker.org/

Dow, S. C. (2011). Heterodox economics: History and prospects. *Cambridge Journal of Economics*, *35*(6), 1151–1165. https://ideas.repec.org/a/oup/cambje/v35y2011i6p1151-1165.html

Escobar, A. (1995). *Encountering Development: The Making and the Unmaking of the Third World*. Princeton, NJ: Princeton University Press.

Harvey, D. (2006). *Spaces of Global Capitalism: A Theory of Uneven Geographical Development*. London: Verso.

Hettne, B. (2010). *"Development and Security: Origins and Future"*. Security Dialogue 41, no.1 (2010): 31–52.

Horner, R. (2020). Towards a new paradigm of global development? Beyond the limits of international development. *Progress in Human Geography*, *44*(3), 415–436. https://doi.org/10.1177/0309132519836158

Hsiang, E. (2023). *Chinese Investment in Africa: A Reexamination of the Zambian Debt Crisis*, Harvard International Review, 25.JAN.2023, https://hir.harvard.edu/chinese-investment-in-africa-a-reexamination-of-the-zambian-debt-crisis/

Hynes, W., & Scott, S. (2013). The evolution of official development assistance: Achievements, criticisms, and a way forward. *OECD Development Co-operation Working Papers, No. 12*. https://www.oecd.org/dac/financing-sustainable-development/development-finance-standards/Evolution%20of%20ODA.pdf

IFAD (2023) 13 reasons why remittances are important, https://www.ifad.org/en/web/latest/-/13-reasons-why-remittances-are-important Accessed online.

Kelberer, V. (2017). Negotiating crisis: International aid and refugee Policy in Jordan. *Middle East Policy*, *XXiV*(4), 148–165.

Knutsson, B. (2009) The Intellectual History of Development Towards a Widening Potential Repertoire Perspectives, No. 13, pp 1–43, Gothenburg Unviersity.

Kragelund, P. (2010). The potential role of non-traditional donors' aid in Africa. *ICTSD Programme on Competitiveness and Sustainable Development, Issue Paper No. 11*, Geneva: International Centre for Trade and Sustainable Development.

Lu, C. (2023). China is a loan shark with no legs left to break. *Foreign Policy*, May 9. https://foreignpolicy.com/2023/05/09/china-debt-lending-paris-club-bri-development-finance/

Mawdsley, E., Savage, L., & Kim, S.-M. (2014). A 'post-aid world'?. *The Geographical Journal*, *180*, 27–38.

Muggah, R. (2023). Opinion: As Chinese aid slows down, the whole world will feel the pinch. *Devex*. https://www.devex.com/news/opinion-as-chinese-aid-slows-down-the-whole-world-will-feel-the-pinch-105359

Murray, W. E., & Overton, J. (2011). Neoliberalism is dead, long live neoliberalism: Neostructuralism and the new international aid regime of the 2000s. Progress in Development Studies, *11*(4): 307–19.

Naylor, T. (2011). Deconstructing development: The use of power and pity in the international development discourse. *International Studies Quarterly*, *55*(1), 177–197.

Ndlovu-Gatsheni, S. J. (2021). Revisiting Marxism and decolonization through the legacy of Samir Amin. *Review of African Political Economy, 48*(167), 50–65.

OECD – DAC. (2022). *Aid at a Glance, Development Finance.* https://www.oecd.org/development/financing-sustainable-development/development-finance-data/aid-at-a-glance.htm

OECD. (2006). *DAC in dates, The History of OECD's Development Assistance Committee.* Paris: OECD.

OECD. (2022). *Development Co-operation Profiles.* Paris: OECD Publishing. https://www.oecd.org/dac/financing-sustainable-development/development-finance-data/aid-at-a-glance.htm

OECD (2023a), *Net ODA (indicator).* doi: 10.1787/33346549-en

OECD. (2023b). *ODA Levels in 2022 – Preliminary Data Detailed Summary Note.* Paris: OECD.

Öhm, M. (2021). Towards geopolitical german development cooperation? Recent history, current trends, and future prospects. *Ifri, Notes du Cerfa*, No. 165, July 2021.

Peet, R., & Hartwick, E. (2015). *Theories of Development: Contentions, Arguments, Alternatives* (3rd ed.). New York: Guilford Publications.

Pieterse, J. N. (2010). *Development Theory: Deconstructions/Reconstructions.* Development Theory: Deconstructions/Reconstructions.

Piketty, T. (2020). *Capital and Ideology.* Cambridge, MA: Harvard University Press.

Regilme, S. (2022). United States foreign aid and multilateralism under the trump presidency. *New Global Studies, 17.* https://doi.org/10.1515/ngs-2021-0030

Rist, G. (2003). *The history of development: From western origins to global faith (Expanded ed.).* London: Zed Books.

Rostow, W. W. (1959) "The Stages of Economic Growth." *Economic History Review* 12#1 1959, pp. 1–16.

Sachs, W. (Ed.). (1992). *The Development Dictionary. A Guide to Knowledge as Power.* London: Zed Books.

Said, E. W. (1978). *Orientalism.* New York, Pantheon Books.

Steffen, Will, Katherine Richardson, Johan Rockström, Sarah E. Cornell, Ingo Fetzer, Elena M. Bennett, Reinette Biggs, Stephen R. Carpenter, Wim de Vries, Cynthia A. de Wit, Carl Folke, Dieter Gerten, Jens Heinke, Georgina M. Mace, Linn M. Persson, Veerabhadran Ramanathan, Belinda Reyers, and Sverker Sörlin (2015) Planetary boundaries: Guiding human development on a changing planet, SCIENCE, 15 Jan 2015 Vol 347, Issue 6223.

Trebesch et al. (2023). *Ukraine Data Tracker.* Kiel: Kiel Institute for the World Economy.

UKAI (2023) Update on ODA eligibility of funding for refugees in the UK, 6 September 2023, https://icai.independent.gov.uk/review/update-on-oda-eligibility-of-funding-for-refugees-in-the-uk/

van Norren, D. (2020). The sustainable development goals viewed through gross national happiness, Ubuntu, and Buen Vivir. *International Environment Agreements, 20,* 431–458.

Veltmeyer, H., & Bowles, P. (Eds.). (2021). The Essential Guide to Critical Development Studies (2nd ed.). Routledge.

Ye, M. (2022). The Dragon's gift: An empirical analysis of China's foreign aid in the new century. *International Trade, Politics and Development, 6*(2), 73–86.

Woods, N. (2005). The shifting politics of foreign aid. *International Affairs, 81*(2), 393–409.

World Economic Forum (2023). The Global Risk Report (18th ed.): Insight Report. Cologny/Geneva: World Economic Forum.

5 The Geopoliticisation of Aid

Introduction

Geopolitical considerations are taking a central role in the aid programmes offered by major donors. While this has likely been the case throughout history, particularly during the Cold War the world is currently witnessing a resurgence of competitive aid strategies. Donors may claim that their primary goal is poverty alleviation, but in this chapter, the discussion delves into the nature of these geopolitical motives and examines some of the criticisms regarding the impact of aid provided. Two case studies are presented, focusing on Africa and the South Pacific, to uncover the geopolitical underpinnings of various donors' aid programmes. Throughout the discussion it becomes evident that aid is increasingly wielded as a tool in the fierce rivalry between the USA and China, even though most recipient nations are keen to remain neutral and avoid taking sides in this conflict. This chapter addresses classical critical and neoliberal geopolitics, as well as issues concerning geoeconomics in a context of development and foreign aid, and presents two case studies focussing on Africa and the South Pacific.

Geopolitics – Classical and Critical

As noted in Chapter 3, the academic study of geopolitics, which is usually attributed to Sir Halford Mackinder's 1904 paper on the concept of the 'Heartland', fell in disrepute because of the ways in which these ideas were adopted by Nazi Germany. However, more recently geopolitics has emerged to become an important area of study, but it has undergone considerable change since the early days of the 20th century. Geography matters fundamentally in human affairs, notwithstanding our hubris about our technological prowess and ability to cover huge distances very easily. At the height of the euphoria about the impact of globalisation, Friedman (2005) declared that the world was 'flat', flattened by new communications technologies, outsourcing strategies by multinational corporations and the creation of global supply chains,

DOI: 10.4324/9781003409946-5

until it resembled one vast level playing field. To many this line of argument always appeared fanciful, but it now seems positively misguided. Mountains still act as important barriers to human interaction and can be used for protection by communities (Scott, 2009).

By contrast, river valleys often act as zones of interaction and cooperation, while marine environments and archipelagos can encourage the development of intensive patterns of trade. Patterns of resource endowment are, of course, extremely important in determining many aspects of economic activity. Rainfall and soil fertility still have a major influence on the viability of agriculture, while the existence of mineral resources can act as a catalyst for industrial growth. All of these factors have an important impact on population growth and on demographic structure more generally. Complex interactions between geography, history, population, culture, politics and economic change are still important – some have even argued that the fate of a nation is essentially determined by its geography. Drawing on the experiences of conflict in Vietnam, Iraq, Afghanistan and elsewhere, Kaplan (2012), in a controversial book, has argued that geography will always have a major influence on strategic realities as well as on broader aspects of human life: geography, he asserts, will always trump globalisation.

Mackinder's (1890) original concepts can be regarded as an early statement of what we would now call *classical geopolitics*, concerned with the control of territory, power and the role of geographical factors in the rise, consolidation and fall of empires. Although Mackinder never used the term geopolitics, he wrote particularly about the ways in which control of the giant landmass of Eurasia was essential to global dominance, which at the time was a revolutionary idea, in that it rated land armies as being more important than the naval capacities that had been so central to the growth of the British Empire. Even before Mackinder set down some of the basic concepts of geopolitics, the major powers had been putting these into practice in the development of their foreign policies: geography was being used in the service of more effective forms of statecraft. For example, since the age of Catherine the Great, Russia had been pushing out the boundaries of its empire, while the British had been trying to safeguard their own position in India by intervening in Afghanistan – what became known as the 'Great Game' (Hopkirk, 1990). The modern revival of interest in geopolitics has been attributed to the adoption of many of these classical ideas by President Richard Nixon and his Secretary of State Henry Kissinger. Their moves to recognise China, intervene in Chile and continue US domination of the oil-rich Middle East were justified in terms of the country's 'geopolitical interests' (Agnew, 2003).

Similarly, the former US National Security Advisor Zbigniew Brzezinski (2004) argued that the way to guarantee US leadership in the preservation of global security was to build a robust US-led network of alliances. This theme of building influence and partnership in various parts of the globe is a recurring theme in classical geopolitics, considered later in this chapter. More recently, such approaches to US foreign policy have regularly reappeared in Washington, for example, in the guise of the 'Neocons', who became increasingly disillusioned with what they saw as a weak US approach to international relations. They advocated a hardline approach that involved the use of overwhelming military power where necessary. The Neocons attained their greatest influence during the Presidency of George W. Bush and successfully advocated military intervention in Afghanistan and Iraq (Gordon & Trainor, 2006).

At a more fundamental level, Kearns (2006) has drawn on three of the basic tenets of Mackinder's thesis and argued that these are equally applicable to current American doctrines as expressed in visions such as the New American Century. The world, he asserted, was facing an important historical rupture that demanded decisive action in the face of a current crisis; in an increasingly globalised world no part of the world could be ignored and left to its own devices; and world powers are locked in a zero-sum game that will be decided by territorial strategies to control critically important resources. For Mackinder, British imperialism was a rationally directed force of nature that was morally obliged to take up the burden of civilising and improving the lives of those not fortunate enough to be British. For Kearns, then, the comparisons with current US thinking are very clear, at a time when the world is facing a crisis, indeed, a polycrisis, every bit is as serious as those facing Britain in 1904.

It is not just in the USA that doctrines derived from classical geopolitics have been prominent in the framing foreign policy. Indeed, these concepts have been one of the hallmarks of great power politics (Mearsheimer, 2001). In post-Soviet Russia, especially under the leadership of Vladimir Putin, foreign policy has been characterised by a pursuit of the lands lost following the breakup of the Soviet Union (henceforth USSR), culminating in the invasion of Ukraine. This appears to be very much in the tradition of Catherine the Great. Indeed, as Bassin and Aksenov (2006) have argued, Mackinder's original Heartland thesis has a particular appeal, pointing as it does to the historical role that the core of Eurasia has played in world affairs.

The methodologies and assumptions adopted in classical geopolitics have come under increasing scrutiny, so much so that a whole new area of study – *critical geopolitics* – has emerged. Classical geopolitics was criticised as being too deterministic and positivist in its approach, and too concerned with a static and limited view of both power and the influence of a number of geographical factors (Agnew, 2003). The new critical geopolitics, by contrast, drew on the more complex concepts of power advanced by postmodern theorists such as Gramsci and Foucault and saw the geographical influences in more sophisticated and fluid terms, stressing the ways in which spatial relations can interact with foreign policy in a mutually constitutive fashion

(Dodds, 2000; Ó Tuathail & Dalby, 1998). In classical geopolitics the features of physical geography were fixed, and constant in their influence on world affairs, but in critical geopolitics space is constantly being made and remade as new factors – such as new technologies – come into play. Arguably, classical geopolitics dealt with the way in which the world was, rather than as it might become in a more desirable future. Others have made this contrast more in disciplinary terms: classical geopolitics was the creature of political science and realist concepts of foreign policy, while critical geopolitics emerged from new currents in geography.

Unsurprisingly, given the nature of Mackinder's original contribution to debates about priorities for British imperial policies, there has been much attention in critical geopolitics to the ways in which large nations have used their power to dominate and exploit subjected peoples (Agnew & Corbridge, 1995). This approach has refocussed attention on the nature of imperialism in the modern era, and the extent to which new empires are similar to others across the ages. Inevitably, most attention has been given to the USA, and the frequent claims made by its leaders that the USA does not have an empire at all, and that its relations with other countries in its orbit are solely aimed at spreading enlightenment, prosperity and democracy. However, Chhachhi and Herrara (2007), for example, insist that there is nothing new about the American Empire – it is like earlier empires all about the exercise of power, control of resources and markets – and the claims of an overriding mandate to bring enormous benefits to all subjects echo the justifications made for British imperialism in an earlier age. Similarly, Slater (2007) argues that the claims of bringing democracy and self-determination to the world ring hollow.

The approaches used in the two branches of geopolitics, classical and critical, can be seen as quite distinct, but it has been argued that it might be possible to gain some useful insights from both. Kelly (2006) has insisted that as a political scientist he sees classical geopolitics as offering the superior insight into the world as it is, but he still sees that much value can be derived from the approaches used in critical geopolitics in casting a clear light on the shortcomings of the classical school. Such a hybrid approach can also alert one to the fact that over time the precise nature of geopolitical imperatives can change, and that some foreign policy decisions may be based on several geopolitical considerations, not all of them pulling in the same direction. Others have attempted to create whole new strands of geopolitics. Several scholars have suggested frameworks for an explicitly Marxist geopolitics, most based on David Harvey's (1982) analysis of the 'spatial fixes' that emerge from the (usually temporary) geographical resolution of capitalist crises.

As Harvey puts it, centres exploit peripheries, metropoli exploit hinterlands, the first world exploits the third to create underdevelopment, and class struggle develops as the struggle of peripheral class formations against the central source of oppression. Such themes are, of course, central to much of the critical geopolitics literature, but some authors have gone further. Colás and Pozo (2011), for example, have focussed on the value of territory to capital, focussing on three levels of abstractions at which territory is valorised by capital – social infrastructure, class conflict and ground-rent proper – and illustrate the value of such a framework in relation to energy disputes between Russia and Ukraine. More recently, there has been some discussion of Confucian geopolitics as a more idealistic alternative to the hard-nosed approach of classical geopolitics in particular. Kong (2021) has suggested that concepts central to Confucianism, such as harmony and multipolarity, might usefully be incorporated into the formulation of foreign policy, although she does suggest that in Chinese external relations there seems to be a large gap between theory and practice, something which is explored later in relation to China's aid programme.

Geopolitics, Geoeconomics and Neoliberal Geopolitics

At the end of the Cold War, in a mistaken belief that the world was entering a new era of peace and stability, Luttwak (1990) suggested that the role of the military in the world was declining while the dominance of commerce was now likely; hence, the old modes of thought about geopolitics could be superseded by *geoeconomics*. For some this might mean the dawn of a world in which territorial issues would become irrelevant: business imperatives would be the sole concern. However, as Luttwak correctly warned, this was never a certain outcome in a world in which national entities and their governments remained supreme. States have always been determined to retain exclusive control over their territories; hence, in the new era of geoeconomics the aim of state actors remains the same as always, only the tools were modified. Thus, it could be argued that geoeconomics now expresses the logic of war in the grammar of commerce. The state has now been seen by economic interest groups as an instrument that can be used both internally and internationally to advance their sectional interests.

This kind of argument has been taken a stage further by Cowen and Smith (2009), who also see a transition taking place towards the increasing influence of economic priorities, but the imperatives flowing from the War on Terror that has arisen at the same time have added an important layer of complexity. Terrorist threats have intensified demands for border control and security at the same time that business groups have been urging governments to make cross-border movements of capital, trade and workers less restricted. But perhaps the most illuminating part of their argument is the insistence that geopolitical issues have become central to the conversations taking place in society, and that the tenor of these dialogues has been subtly changed over time. For example, during the Cold War, geopolitical concerns became integral to societal concerns, creating what they call the 'geopolitical social', but that is now being transformed into the 'geoeconomic social'. Increasingly,

governments are seeing themselves as players in the economy, both nation-
ally and internationally, and as formerly government services are privatised
the distinctions between the private and the public sectors become increasingly blurred.

Other authors, observing the growing salience of economic affairs in the
arguments around geopolitics, have introduced the term *neoliberal geopolitics*. Certainly, both examine similar contemporary trends, such as privatisation and the primacy given to market mechanisms, that are central to the
neoliberal paradigm. However, there is perhaps a harder edge to strategies of
neoliberal geopolitics, bringing together traditional geopolitics with uncom-
promising market fundamentalism. Roberts et al. (2003) suggest that for the
true neoliberal believers it is the non-incorporation into the global market of
some nations that represents a potent challenge to international wellbeing and
security. In the late 1990s pressure from Wall Street resulted in a campaign
by the US government to force South Korea to remove its restrictions on the
access of foreign banks to its local capital markets. Reluctantly South Korea
complied, and the result was a massive inflow of foreign capital followed by
the rapid withdrawal of these funds, one of the key factors in the Asian Financial Crisis of 1997 (McKay, 2003; Sparke, 2018).

In the crude version of geopolitics, as practised in the 19th century, the aim
was the acquisition of territory and resources in order to accumulate wealth.
The aim now is to accumulate wealth by controlling markets and to maximise
international competitiveness rather than simply adding imperial possessions.
Borders between the local, the internal and the international are being blurred.
Governments seek to promote competitiveness on the international market
through government programmes which usually operate both within the nation and at the international scale through various export activities (cf. Moisio
& Paasi, 2013a, 2013b).

Power – Hard and Soft

One important conclusion to be derived from the preceding discussion is that
the study of geopolitics is about comprehending the geographies of security
and power. This raises the vital question of how we understand the nature and
limits of power in the modern world and how that power is wielded by various
state actors. At the most general level, power is often defined as the capability
to induce others to behave in a manner that the wielder of the power prefers.
For centuries there have been debates about the most effective way to achieve
this influence. Machiavelli put the question this way: is it better to be loved
or feared? In the modern world this is now framed as the choice between hard
and soft power. Traditionally, power was measured in strictly military terms,
including a nation's ability to wage war, the capacity to create fear through a
large army or navy, destructive weapons or the possession of economic weapons that can either buy compliance or threaten economic ruin.

On the other hand, Nye (1990, 2004), who is usually credited to have coined the terms, has defined soft power as 'the ability to shape the preferences of others', which is often shaped by some intangible attraction that persuades people to go along with others without any explicit fear of punishment or expectation of reward. He argues that the nature of power in the modern world is changing, and that soft power is often more effective and less costly. As to whether it is better to be loved or feared, he suggests that it is usually best to be both, but what is often dangerous is the use of hard power without some attempt to build some supporting soft power.

The existing polycrisis is closely aligned with Nye's *smart power* which is a concept combining elements of both soft power and hard power and the aim to achieve foreign policy objectives. It emphasises the strategic and adaptive use of various tools, including diplomacy, economic assistance, military capabilities and cultural influence, based on the specific context and desired outcomes. In the context of development aid during a polycrisis, smart power in the form of development aid can be an effective approach. It involves leveraging a combination of soft power and hard power elements to address the immediate needs of affected populations, promote long-term stability and advance broader development goals by supporting developing countries throughout the moment of polycrisis.

Geopolitics, Development and Foreign Aid: Geopolitics Meets Development

The rediscovery of geopolitics has generated a significant literature in recent years, and similarly interest in development issues continues to be significant; however, the intersection between the two concepts has rarely been discussed. For the most part, the study of development has been seen as a largely technical issue, usually involving the economics or institutional dynamics of poor countries, while geopolitics has dealt with – at least in the popular mind – relationships between nation states. There have, however, been a small number of studies arguing that in the modern world geopolitical considerations now have a significant impact on how development priorities are evaluated, and the aim here is to build on these insights and to explore how these mechanisms are at work in various parts of the world. Central to the narrative here is a dialogue that took place in response to an article by Slater (1993), in which he explored the notion of *the geopolitical imagination* and how it is central to the ways in which the aims and strategies of development are conceptualised.

Successive waves of Western development thought have essentially been responses to changing geopolitical conditions as perceived through an imperial will to power, with geopolitical imperatives providing a frame for the construction of a world map of competing blocs, the interactions between them and a development agenda for each. Thus, for much of the Cold War era the contest between the West and the USSR necessitated a division of the globe into three worlds: the First World of the West, a Communist Second World and a largely 'underdeveloped' Third World (see also Hettne, 1990). The West as heir to the Enlightenment was the most civilised and superior region, enjoying a system of democracy that was preferable to the dictatorship found in the Communist world and possessing the technologies and modern systems that needed to be diffused to the Third World, a premise that gave rise to the modernisation theory that was dominant in development thought during this period. Poverty was to be ended through the complete transformation and modernisation of 'Third World'.

Similarly, Slater (1993) argues, the rise to dominance during the 1980s by the neoliberal paradigm reflected the geopolitical and geoeconomic priorities of that time and involved an emphasis in development policy on the benefits of globalisation that could be garnered by states with small but efficient governments being able to harness the benefits of markets at all levels. Comments on this article were made by Ó Tuathail (1998), who, while supporting Slater's basic argument, attempted to radicalise the approach by deconstructing the term geopolitics. This area of analysis, he suggests, does indeed revolve around the nations state, its roles and powers and the relationships between states, but geopolitics should be placed alongside and contrasted with *geopolitics*, the contest between different political ideas, ideals and aspirations. The aim should be the liberation of development thinking from repressive and exploitative forms of geopolitical imagination, and replacing them with a vision of how the world might be structured, along with a new and complementary development theory, as canvassed at various points in this book. In his rejoinder to Ó Tuathail and particularly in some of his later writings Slater (1994, 1997, 2007) takes his argument a stage further, insisting that dominant theories of development are tailored to meet the sources of perceived threats at any particular moment. During the Cold War, the threat came from the USSR and the emphasis was on modernisation to reduce any attraction that Communist Systems might have for the 'Third World'. Later, in the War on Terror, development ideas were designed to counter the threats that might originate in poorly organised states, hence the emphasis on the development of 'good governance'. The names were also changed after the Cold War, with the Three Worlds being replaced by the Global North/Global South division. The Third World and the Global South signified the 'underdeveloped' part of the world, but the approach to 'developing' them was rather different, the new approach being determined by the changing geopolitical situation.

Slater's argument is persuasive, but it could be added that when intervention was seen as necessary, especially during the Cold War, developmental goals were often manipulated or even misrepresented to provide a more palatable justification. In the early stages, significant amounts of foreign aid were provided but more significant in the long term were the willingness to accept large volumes of exports from these countries, something that would be impossible in the current climate of economic nationalism. In all of these countries the role of a strong interventionist state was central; however, this success was portrayed in official circles as yet another example of free markets at work. This was clearly untrue, but this narrative was supportive of the 'Western Way'.

Geopolitics and Foreign Aid After 1945: The Cold and the War on Terror

In all foreign aid programmes there are a variety of motivations at work, and it would be cynical to dismiss the presence of a genuine desire to assist nations in their quest for development; nevertheless, it is probably true that in almost all aid geopolitical factors are also at work. The nature of geopolitical priorities changes over time, and this has important ramifications for the precise development goals that are prioritised and hence the form of aid that is provided. For example, in the immediate aftermath of the World War II the first priority was the reconstruction of Europe and Japan, notably through the Marshall Plan in Europe. The clear aim was economic reconstruction providing export markets for the USA and the rapid improvement in lifestyles in order to demonstrate that revolution and a turn to Communism were not necessary for the achievement of prosperity. Rostow's (1960) influential message was clear: 'take off' could be achieved in a series of changes.

The enormously successful programme that was put in place to assist South Korea after the Korean War and this achievement was held up by the West as proof of the superiority of Rostow's methods. At the same time the USSR was pouring resources into North Korea in an attempt to demonstrate the advantages of the Communist system. More generally, Western aid in the 1960s and 1970s was aimed at what came to be known as *modernisation*, the achievement of development within a capitalist framework through the adoption of superior technologies and modes of organisation transferred from the West in part through foreign aid initiatives. USSR aid also offered superior technologies and know-how but set within a non-capitalist society, and with trade patterns tied to the USSR and its allies. Beginning in the late 1960s China also began to provide a development model, followed soon by a Chinese aid programme.

The approaches taken by the USA and the USSR to the use of their aid programmes to seek influence especially in the Third World, a direction also supported by the former colonial powers and US allies Britain and France, allowed many governments in smaller and poorer countries to play off each side against the other to gain greater support. However, there is evidence that aid given for essentially political purposes is rarely effective in generating real long-term development benefits, and this seems to have been especially true in the period after 1970 (Lee, 2022; Reinsberg, 2019).

The fall of the Berlin Wall in 1989, followed by the breakup of the USSR in 1991, marked a geopolitical watershed, with enormous consequences for foreign aid. The Cold War was replaced by a unipolar moment in which, at least for the time being, the USA was the unchallenged superpower. There was a double squeeze on aid: the end of superpower rivalry meant that the amount of aid on offer was reduced, while at the same time nations in the South were no longer able to extract aid from both sides. For some countries that had firmly tied themselves to the USSR – notably Cuba and North Korea – this was a disaster, as financial support and guaranteed access to Comecon markets disappeared. During this time neoliberalism was consolidated as the dominant ideology across most of the countries of the North, with serious ramifications for the development model being encouraged in the Global South. The aid emphasis was on promoting globalisation and free trade, and on transforming economic structures and government activities to ensure that 'markets would work for the poor'. Aid became increasingly conditional on governments in the South undertaking programmes of structural adjustment that involved the large-scale privatisation of government services, the removal of many tariffs and restrictions on imports and the acceptance of foreign investment in previously restricted areas. Many of these governments had little choice because access to emergency budget support from the IMF was dependent on the implementation of such structural adjustment reforms.

A further geopolitical turning point took place in 2001with the terrorist attacks on the USA and the implementation of the War on Terror. Emphasis shifted to the support of governments, particularly in certain regions deemed to be unstable and hence likely to provide havens for terrorist organisations. In the wake of the US attacks on Afghanistan and the removal of the Taliban regime, Pakistan became a key theatre in the battle against extremism. In the decade immediately after 9/11 Pakistan received some $18 billion in US aid, predominantly military support. Economic sanctions that had been imposed when Pakistan tested its nuclear device in 1998 were removed, but it soon became clear that this increase in aid was not having the desired results. In 2009 President Obama argued that extremism would not be defeated by bullets and bombs alone, but through genuine development and increases in incomes. Hence, the emphasis on military aid was replaced with a much more broadly based aid programme designed to deliver hearts and minds to the cause of enhanced security in the region. However, Mumtaz (2013) argued that even this revised aid programme failed to deliver the results desired by the USA, largely because the general security milieu was not a conducive one: the security aims of the USA were not in line with those of the Pakistan government or with popular opinion.

The War on Terror still exists, with no clear end in sight, and in spite of some serious setbacks, neoliberalism and globalisation are still the ruling ideologies in the developed world. However, an important new factor has emerged into the geopolitical calculus of both rich and poor countries: the rise of China and the re-emergence of superpower competition made more complex by the growing security and economic cooperation between China and Russia as the result of the Ukraine war. This new geopolitical reality is ensuring that the ruling ideas on international development and the aid initiatives that are designed to support it are being fundamentally transformed, culminating in a new reality.

The Geopoliticisation of Aid: The Current Era

In recent years we have seen international developments that amount to something akin to the Cold War, and many of the foreign policies of the protagonists mirror the stances that characterised that earlier era, including foreign aid programmes. In Chapter 3, we have already set out the major contours of this new Cold War: the military, economic, ideological and technological competition between the USA and China; the close level of military and economic cooperation between China and Russia; and the war in Ukraine, with determined efforts by the USA and its European allies to stand firm against the Russian invasion of Ukraine. But there are also some features of the current geopolitical environment that are more novel. Chapter 4 identified the complexity in thinking about international development and the most appropriate methods for realising gains in the Global South which are far more uncertain than in the earlier Cold War era. In many nations of the Global South, which for long had to endure the sufferings resulting from the imposition of IMF structural adjustment programmes, there is now a determination to have much more say in how the goals and methods of development are to be formulated. Part of this involves a greater emphasis on South-South cooperation and the search for regional solutions to economic and strategic challenges.

The Middle East remains the major locus of the War on Terror, but some of the oil-rich nations in the region are now emerging as more active international players and aid donors. There is also reluctance by some smaller nations to take sides in this new version of the Cold War. In Asia, for example, almost all countries have China as their major trading partner and would similarly have a great deal to lose from alienating the USA, so they are walking a very fine line. There may even be some nostalgia for the Non-Aligned Movement that similarly defined the Third World as being allied with neither the First nor the Second Worlds. These processes, both old and new, operate differently in particular contexts. To illustrate these trends towards the geopoliticisation, two case studies are advanced – Africa and the South Pacific.

Africa: The Battle for Hearts and Minds....
and Resources

The plundering of Africa's resources by outside powers has a long history. For example, the colonial period, dating from the 1880s when the 'scramble for

Africa' carved up the continent and allocated pieces to the various European powers, is still a vivid memory and one which conditions current responses to foreign initiatives. It is in this context that the competition for influence in Africa is so fierce that it has been labelled 'the new scramble for Africa'. Africa has some 154 nations and thus has a strong voice in the United Nations and similar organisations, giving attempts to woo African hearts and minds an important geopolitical dimension. Africa also has a predominantly young and rapidly expanding population, providing a strong market for foreign exporters. But behind these attractions is the demand of the continent's resources. The former colonial powers still retain a strong interest in the region, but there are now some important new players. China's aggressive involvement in many African countries is exciting most interest, and Russia is now staking a somewhat surprising claim. Furthermore, there is considerable interest in the region in formulating a more independent and authentically African model of development. The role that the BRICS block is now playing is very relevant here.

The precise level of total aid flowing into Africa is difficult to ascertain, largely because Chinese aid is not part of the DAC system and the data on many components of its assistance to Africa has not been released. It is estimated that in 2022 aid to Africa from the DAC countries was some $34 billion, a significant reduction from the 2021 level; however, it is difficult to obtain figures particularly on Chinese loans to Africa, and the terms under which they have be granted. China's arrival as a major aid donor has raised a number of questions relating particularly to the aims of this large aid programme, the impact it is having in the receiving countries and the extent to which Chinese aid is different from assistance given by the traditional Western donors.

For the critics of Chinese aid, the aim of Beijing is to draw African countries into a web of unsustainable debt and use this leverage to gain access to Africa's immense natural resources, to a number of strategically important facilities, and to prop up authoritarian leaders favourable to it. For a number of years China has been touted as a transformative and generous trade and investment partner, offering the possibility of a 'New Silk Road' for Africa. However, several commentators have expressed strong reservations. Carmody and Taylor (2010) argue that China's approaches to African elites vary depending on local geography and history, and in some cases the use of soft power is appropriate, while in other cases blatant hard power – economic, political and military – is preferred. They label this approach 'flexigemony' and contrast it with the undifferentiated approach of the USA, which pushes for market-oriented policies in all circumstances, to achieve neoliberal outcomes. They also suggest that this blending of hard and soft power is akin to Nye's notion of 'smart power'. In Sudan, they suggest, hard military and economic force has been used through the supply of military aid and support for autocratic regimes, to deadly effect. Zambia, on the other hand, has moved much more towards democracy, but even here blatant economic coercion has been adopted, through the provision of loans and through the activities of the 200 or so Chinese companies now operating in the country.

Much has been made of China's Belt and Road Initiative (BRI) with its promise of delivering some massive and much-needed infrastructure projects to African nations starved of capital for decades. However, there have been numerous criticisms of this programme, as essentially designed to focus on trade flows and the supply of resources back to China, which is essentially a continuation of the old colonial pattern of exploitation. Because of growing debt levels, but also in response to some local misgivings, several African nations have cancelled BRI projects. China itself, because of its own economic problems, has dramatically scaled back its investments in BRI projects. Nevertheless, China is positioning itself as an alternative to the IMF as a lender of last resort. Although the interest rates and the length of the repayment period are rather less attractive than those offered by the IMF, some African countries have been attracted by Beijing's refusal to impose IMF style economic, political or governance conditions on any loans.

These are serious criticisms, but they are certainly not shared by all commentators. China's unwillingness to attach conditions to its financial support, seen by some as a problem, can also be interpreted as positive. Unconditional aid of this kind has been welcomed by Gilpin (2023), since it challenges the ability of the tradition Western donors to shape the development strategies of African nations. This represents a challenge to the existing neoliberal world order, which is a good thing, she argues. African leaders can thus be free to explore new ideas, ones more in line with the priorities and realities of their own nations, and if necessary, delink their economies from an essentially exploitative global order. Other writers have suggested that while China does certainly use its aid for its own benefit and to create opportunities for its own companies, this has been standard procedure for Western donors for decades (Harchaoui et al., 2021). It is probably a measure of the way that foreign aid in Africa has been geopoliticised that both sides attempt to denigrate the motives of the others and cast doubts on the effectiveness of their aid, and as a result any chance of cooperative efforts and learning form the mistakes of others is lost.

Finally, the new role of Russia in Africa needs our attention, for it is something that is certainly causing problems for the West. Partly in response to the Western alliance against Russia in the war in Ukraine, Russia is now seeking more influence in various parts of Africa. The Wagner mercenary group provided assistance to a number of leaders, and at the time of writing the situation in Niger is dangerous. Following an army coup against the elected ruler, President Mohamed Bazoum, the USA, France and other West African nations have threatened military intervention to restore democracy, but in the large demonstrations in support of the coup leaders Russian flags have been prominent and appeals for help have been made to Vladimir Putin. It is also interesting to note that the Russian Orthodox Church now has a presence in Niger and elsewhere in the Sahel.

The South Pacific: A New Competition for Influence

Many of the same issues are also coming to the fore in the new area of competition for influence and strategic advantage emerging in the islands of the South Pacific. For decades this has been a calm area seen as the area of influence of Australia, New Zealand and the USA, but this has been disturbed by China, presenting itself as a new donor. The region has few minerals of interest to outsiders, but it has enormous fish resources, and above all it has enormous strategic value sitting between the USA and East Asia, and is on the doorstep of Australia and New Zealand, both of which are US allies. Western alarm has been triggered in particular by agreements made between China and the Solomon Islands, Vanuatu and Papua New Guinea to increase cooperation and training in policing. This has been interpreted by the West as being too close to defence cooperation. The result is that aid to the region from Australia and the USA has increased sharply after a long period of what both countries recognise as serious neglect. The USA has also opened a number of new embassies in the region, while Australia has expanded opportunities for people from the Pacific to work temporarily in Australia.

There has been little research on Chinese aid to the Pacific, largely because the presence of China in the region is relatively new. However, one study by Jurriaan, et al. (2021) suggests that many of the myths about Chinese aid are not supported by the evidence. It is not clear that Beijing is trying to create an 'debt trap', nor are funds directed to those island states that have been relatively friendly to China in UN voting patterns, for example. However, the authors stress that much more research is needed on aid programmes and their effectiveness in this new arena of geopolitical competition.

One policy area that is acting as a severe handicap for Australia and the USA relates to climate change. As sea levels rise, it appears inevitable that some islands will be completely inundated; hence, there is much interest in programmes to mitigate temperature rises, and established developed nations are being blamed for a lack of action. The South Pacific Forum has for a number of years tried to put pressure on Australia, a member of the group, to adopt much more ambitious targets. China, by contrast, is generally seen as being much more active in environmental policy and this gives it a major advantage.

As in Africa, some newcomers are now entering the aid business. Saudi Arabia has recently announced a grant to the Solomon Islands to support the upcoming South Pacific Games to be held in Honiara, an event that China is also supporting through the construction of a stadium. The Pacific, once seen as a leisurely backwater, has now been drawn into a global contest for influence, resources, markets and strategic advantage, demonstrating that no part of the globe is removed from geopolitically motivated moves and countermoves in which aid is now central.

A Concluding Note

Aid programmes from all of the major donors are becoming more geopoliticised: aid is given predominantly to buy political support, gain access to markets or acquire valuable energy and mineral resources. At the same time, most countries receiving aid are most reluctant to take sides, particularly in the intense economic and strategic competition between the USA and China. This represents a dangerous new phase in which the very definition of development and the role of aid in achieving true change are being subordinated to geopolitical objectives: unfortunately, aid is now in the process of being weaponised.

References

Agnew, J. (2003). *Geopolitics: Re-visioning World Politics* (2nd ed.). Milton Park: Routledge.

Agnew, J., & Corbridge, S. (1995). *Mastering Space: Hegemony, Territory and International Political Economy*. Milton Park: Routledge.

Bassin, M., & Aksenov, K. (2006). Mackinder and the heartland theory in post-Soviet Geopolitical Discourse. *Geopolitics*, *11*(1), 99–118.

Blair, R., Robert, M., & Roessler, P. (2022). Foreign aid and soft power: Great power competition in Africa in the early twenty-first century. *British Journal of Political Science*, *52*, 1355–1376.

Brzezinski, Z. (2004). *The Choice: Global Domination or Global Leadership*. New York: Basic Books.

Callinicos, A. (2007). Does capitalism need the state system? *Cambridge Review of International Affairs*, *20*(4), 533–549.

Carmody, P., & Taylor, I. (2010). Flexigemony and force in China's resource diplomacy in Africa: Sudan and Zambia Compared. *Geopolitics*, *15*, 496–515.

Chhachhi, A., & Herrera, L. (2007). Empire, geopolitics and development. *Development & Change*, *38*(6), 1021–1040.

Colás, A., & Pozo, G. (2011). The value of territory: Towards a marxist geopolitics. *Geopolitics*, *16*(1), 211–220.

Cowen, D., & Smith, N. (2009). After geopolitics? From the geopolitical social to geoeconomics. *Antipode*, *41*(1), 22–48.

Dodds, K. (2000). *Geopolitics in a Changing World*. Hoboken, NJ: Prentice Hall.

Dodds, K., & Sidaway, J. (1994). Locating critical geopolitics. *Environment and Planning D: Society & Space*, *12*, 515–524.

Friedman, T. (2005). *The World is Flat: A Brief History of the Twenty-First Century*. New York: Farrar, Straus & Giroux.

Gilpin, S. (2023). China, Africa and the international aid system: A challenge to (the Norms Underpinning) the neoliberal world order? *Journal of Asian and African Studies*, *58*(3), 277–297.

Gordon, M., & Trainor, B. (2006). *Cobra II: The Inside Story of the Invasion and Occupation of Iraq*. New York: Pantheon.

Harchaoui, T., Maseland, R., & Watkinson, J. (2021). Carving out an empire? How China strategically uses aid to facilitate Chinese business expansion in Africa. *Journal of African Economies, 30*(2), 183–204.

Harvey, D. (1982). *The Limits to Capital*. Oxford: Basil Blackwell.

Hettne, B. (1990). *Development Theory and the Three Worlds*. New York: Longman.

Hopkirk, P. (1990). *The Great Game: On Secret Service in High Asia*. London: John Murray.

Jonas, A. (2013). City-regionalism as a contingent 'Geopolitics of Capitalism'. *Geopolitics, 18*(2), 284–297.

Jurriaan, B., Grieken, V., & Kantorowicz, J. (2021). Debunking myths about China: The determinants of China's official financing to the Pacific. *Geopolitics, 26*(3), 861–888.

Kaplan, R. (2012). *The Revenge of Geography: What the Map Tells Us About Coming Conflicts and the Battle Against Fate*. New York: Random House.

Kearns, G. (2006). Naturalising Empire: Echoes of mackinder for the next American Century? *Geopolitics, 11*(1), 74–98.

Kelly, P. (2006). A critique of critical geopolitics. *Geopolitics, 11*(1), 24–53.

Kong, L. (2021). A journey of a thousand miles begins with a single step: Towards a confucian geopolitics. *Dialogues in Human Geography, 11*(2), 253–256.

Lee, J. (2022). Foreign aid, development, and US strategic interests in the cold war. *International Studies Quarterly, 66*, 1–14.

Luttwak, E. (1990). From geopolitics to geo-economics: Logic of conflict, grammar of commerce. *The National Interest, 20*, 17–23.

McKay, J. (2003). The restructuring of the Korean economy Since 1986 and the onset of the financial crisis: The industrial-financial nexus. In T. MoonJoong & C. Sok-Suh (Eds.), *The Korean Economy at the Crossroads* (pp. 69–83). London: Routledge.

Mackinder, H. J. (1890). The physical basis of political geography. *Scottish Geographical Magazine, 6*(2), 78–84.

Mandon, P., & Woldmichael, T. (2022). *Has Chinese Aid Benefited Recipient Countries?* Washington DC: International Monetary Fund, Working Paper WP22/46.

Mearsheimer, J. (2001). *The Tragedy of Great Power Politics*. New York: W.W. Norton.

Milner, H., & Tingley, D. (2013). *The Geopolitics of Foreign Aid*. Northampton, MA: Edward Elgar.

Moisio, S., & Paasi, A. (2013a). Beyond state-centricity: Geopolitics of changing state space. *Geopolitics, 18*(2), 255–266.

Moisio, S., & Paasi, A. (2013b). From geopolitical to geoeconomic? The changing political rationalities of state Space. *Geopolitics, 18*(2), 267–283.

Mumtaz, K. (2013). Securitization of foreign aid: An analysis of US-Pakistan aid relations Post 9/11. *PRIAD Policy Journal, 1*(1), 2–19.

Murphy, A. (2004). Is there a politics in geopolitics? *Progress in Human Geography, 28*(5), 619–640.

Nye, J. (1990). *Bound to Lead: The Changing Nature of American Power*. New York: Basic Books.

Nye, J. (2004). *Soft Power: The Means to Success in World Politics*. New York: Public Affairs.

O'Hara, S., & Heffernan, M. (2006). From geo-strategy to geo-economics: The 'Heartland' and British imperialism before and after mackinder. *Geopolitics, 11*, 54–73.

Ó Tuathail, G. (1994). Critical geopolitics and development theory: Intensifying the dialogue. *Transactions of the Institute of British Geographers, 19*(2), 228–223.

Ó Tuathail, G. (1998). Postmodern geopolitics? The modern geopolitical imagination and beyond. In G. Ó Tuathail & S. Dalby (Eds.), *Rethinking Geopolitics* (pp. 16–38). London: Routledge.

Ó Tuathail, G., & Agnew, J. (1992). Geopolitics and discourse: Practical geopolitical reasoning in American Foreign Policy. *Political Geography Quarterly, 11*, 155–175.

Ó Tuathail, G., & Dalby, S. (1998). *Rethinking Geopolitics.* London: Routledge.

Petras, J., & Veltmeyer, H. (2002). Age of reverse aid: Neoliberalism as a catalyst of regression. *Development & Change, 33*(2), 281–293.

Power, M., & Mohan, M. (2010). Towards a critical geopolitics of China's engagement with African development. *Geopolitics, 15*, 462–495.

Reinsberg, B. (2019). Do countries use foreign aid to buy geopolitical influence? Evidence from donor campaigns for temporary UN Security council seats. United Nations University, WIDER Working Paper 2019/4.

Roberts, S., Secor, A., & Sparke, M. (2003). Neoliberal geopolitics. *Antipode, 35*(5), 886–897.

Rostow, W. W. (1960). *The Stages of Economic Growth.* Cambridge: Cambridge University Press.

Scott, J. (2009). *The Art of Not Being Governed: An Anarchist History of Upland Southeast Asia.* New Haven, CT: Yale University Press.

Slater, D. (2007). Imperial geopolitics and the promise of democracy. *Development & Change, 38*(6), 1041–1054.

Slater, D. (2010). The imperial present and the geopolitics of power. *Geopolitica(s), 1*(2), 191–205.

Slater, D. (1997). Geopolitical imagination across the North-South divide: Issues of difference, development, and power. *Political Geography, 16*(8), 621–653.

Slater, D. (1994). Reimagining the geopolitics of development: Continuing the dialogue. *Transactions of the Institute of British Geographers, 19*(2), 233–238.

Slater, D. (1993). The geopolitical imagination and the enframing of development theory. *Transactions of the Institute of British Geographers, 18*(4), 419–439.

Slater, D., & Bell, M. (2002). Aid and the geopolitics of the post-colonial: Critical reflections on new labour's overseas development strategy. *Development & Change, 33*(2), 335–361.

Sparke, M. (2018). Globalising capitalism & the dialectics of geopolitics and geoeconomics. *Environment & Planning A: Economy & Space, 50*(2), 484–489.

Starr, H. (2013). On geopolitics: Spaces & places. *International Studies Quarterly, 57*, 433–439.

Stephen, M., & Skidmore, D. (2019). The AIIB and the liberal international order. *Chinese Journal of International Politics, 12*(1), 61–91.

Usman, Z. (2021). *What Do We Know About Chinese Lending to Africa?* Washington, DC: Carnegie Endowment for International Peace.

6 Geopolitical Crises and the Changing Role of Aid

Introduction

The world is in crisis, or as argued in Chapter 1, crises. This book commenced with a conceptualisation of the contemporary context as being a crisis of modernity. Periodic crises seem to be inevitable within a capitalist system. Major events of the late 19th century and of course the great Depression gave rise to a whole new area of economic theory developed by Keynes. The evolution from Keynesianism to neoliberalism shows evidence of enhancing the likelihood of crises, through the financialisation of the economy, and the rolling back of regulations limiting the flow of capital between nations.

Today's world has progressed beyond periodic bounded crises, provoking discourse on polycrisis. Arguably the world is progressing towards a permanent state of geopolitical crises which has all the hallmarks of becoming the new normal. This contrasts with recent crises such as the 2007–2010 Global Financial Crisis, followed by the 2009–2019 European Sovereign Debt Crisis, the 2015 European Migration Crisis, the 2019 ongoing Covid-19 crises and the Persian Gulf crisis (2019–present), to name but a few. These crises differ from the current, insofar as they did not challenge, to any significant extent, the existing world order. They emerged from certain economic, political, humanitarian, environmental, social and health-related cataclysms, which may be classified as large-scale events each having a significant impact on society, the economy, political systems and/or the environment. Some parts of the world seem to have been in almost permanent crisis, and in fact the perception that crisis is the abnormal state identifies the privilege of those for whom crisis is not the norm. However, what has characterised modern crises is that they have been global in nature and have had severe impacts in the Global North as well as the South and hence have been taken more seriously by popular opinion and the media.

The intersection of multiple global crises since the beginning of the 2020s has especially impacted on development aid. The Covid-19 pandemic, the rapid escalation of the Russian-Ukrainian war, a rapidly evolving climate crisis and inherent structural weaknesses have brought about the worst

DOI: 10.4324/9781003409946-6

cost-of-living and food crisis in a generation. These crises have caused massive disruptions to global energy and food markets, and have pushed food, energy and commodity prices to record levels. There is growing evidence that crises are not isolated events but tend to be cumulative in both their causes and in their impacts. Thus, the Asian Crisis of 1997 can be seen as the precursor of the Global Financial Crisis, and the fallout from the GFC is still with us and has interacted in complex ways with more recent events such as the Covid pandemic. The impacts of these crises have been experienced globally, in the Global South, but also amongst vulnerable socio-economic strata in developed countries. Millions of people have been forced into poverty.

However, the current polycrisis, as discussed in previous chapters, is a simultaneous occurrence of multiple crises in succession and compounding geopolitical effects. For example, the Russo-Ukraine military war, which can be further argued to be an economic war, and a propaganda war – all of which are catalysts for political, economic, energy, food, sovereign debt, migration, environmental and defence crises. Cumulatively, these crises have caused massive disruptions to global energy and food markets and have pushed food, energy and commodity prices to record levels and have especially impacted nations of the Global South, and vulnerable groups.

One catalyst for the polycrisis is the military (battlefield) war which is being played out in Ukraine. It is a geopolitical war fought between the West using Ukraine as a proxy and the Russian Federation, which gave an impetus for the economic war which emerged from the sanctions imposed by the West on Russia. Furthermore, since the beginning of the Russian-Ukrainian conflict the latter's economy has significantly suffered due to its territorial losses, infrastructure destruction and trade restrictions. Even before the war Ukraine had difficulties in attracting foreign investment due to its high level of corruption. According to Transparency International (2022) Ukraine ranks 122/180 on the Corruption Perception Index 2022. This militated against economic growth, exacerbated by the invasion. The social crisis is characterised by the displacement of millions of people within Ukraine and beyond its borders and the alleged human rights abuses including violation of freedom of the press and freedom of speech. Finally, the conflict has brought about a global security crisis, with a potential to engulf Russia's and Ukraine's neighbouring EU and NATO countries.

Against this backdrop, there is a compelling argument to be made that the Russo-Ukraine war is a complex and ongoing key contributor to the polycrisis which requires a multifaceted approach to deal with its many interrelated challenges. However, to provide a detailed analysis and discussion is beyond the scope of this chapter. Thus, we will focus on polycrisis as the norm, the economic 'war' and sanctions as drivers of the polycrisis, the concept of geopolitics, before turning back to some of the key findings within which this context becomes even more problematic.

Polycrisis as the Norm

As noted in previous chapters, polycrisis is defined as a phenomenon '…
where disparate crises interact such that the overall impact far exceeds the
sum of each part' (World Economic Forum, 2023, n.p.). There is a compelling
argument to be made that the Russia-Ukraine war, which commenced in 2014,
is a major force of instability, creating significant and far-reaching effects on
multiple areas, including military, political, economic and humanitarian dimensions, deepening complex and ongoing crises. As previously discussed,
there have been a wide array of geopolitical tensions and actions, since the
end of the Second World War (WWII) and throughout the Cold War. Some
examples are the USSR invasion of Hungary in 1956 Czechoslovakia in 1968,
Afghanistan in 1979, the 1948–1949 Berlin Blockade, Cuban Missile Crises
in 1962, the USA-led Vietnam War from 1955 to 1975, the 1950 to 1953
Korean War, the USA-led NATO war in Afghanistan from 2001 to 2021 and
the various wars in the Middle East and North Africa, undertaken directly or
as proxy by USA and its allies, and the Russian Federation, respectively. If
one considers all the post-WWII wars and political, economic, financial and
military crises, it can be argued that crises are normal. However, these crises
were contained to a large extent within specific countries and regions or geopolitical spheres of interests.

However, since 2014, the situation is different. The impact and associated crises of the Russia-Ukraine war go beyond specific countries or regions,
having profound global effects. The current context, however, must not be
confused with an interregnum where the existing normal is vanishing and a
new normal is striving to emerge (Babic, 2020). It appears that polycrisis is
the new normal. Considering the multiple interrelated crises operating in parallel with the Russia-Ukraine war, particularly climate, health, food, energy
and debt crises, it is difficult to argue that the existing neoliberal international
order will re-emerge through renewal and re-organisation.

The causes of more recent periods of crisis are not random events but are
inextricably linked to underlying development in the economy. Under neoliberalism the search for profit and access to new resources has pushed the reach
of the global system into corners of the globe previously isolated and one
result is that infections seen previously as having little contact with humans
are now exposed to greater contact, and this may have been the case with
Covid – although of course there are other theories in this particular case.
Thus, these events are causally related, and can be traced back to the dominant
ideology of neoliberalism. The effect of these forces has been the creation of
multiple interacting crises taking effect at more or less the same time – what
we have called a polycrisis. Similarly, neoliberalism has built into it a vitally
important spirit of competition that has fuelled increasingly fraught relationships between nations. China was opened up economically by US capital as

part of the Cold War strategies to isolate the Soviet Union, but this was so successful that it created an economic and strategic rival to the US that had to be taken seriously when so many US manufacturing jobs had been exported to Asia. The populist backlash resulted in the rise of Donald Trump and the Brexit vote, for example.

One result of this growing competition has seen growing rivalry between Western-style neoliberalism and the state capitalism of China. It is inherent in neoliberalism to seek to extend the vision of free markets to all corners of the globe, and this has resulted in a pushback from both China and Russia. This has been seen recently in the annual meeting of the BRICS in South Africa. The war in Ukraine is of course the most serious manifestation of these global forces.

A pertinent question is therefore what the post-Russia-Ukraine war new normal will be? In response a probable scenario is that the world economy will continue to be plagued by a sequence of political, food, cost-of-living and energy crises and economic wars underpinned by trade and financial sanctions. In short according to the World Economic Forum (2023) the world is facing a period of economic and political instability and polycrisis, a unique, uncertain and turbulent decade to come is their assessment. A world where polycrisis as the norm will most likely be a de-globalising unstable unpredictable and heterogeneous socio-political and socio-economic amalgam, characterised by inconsistent flaws of protectionism, crises of multilateralism and the rise of a variety of political and economic ideologies such as illiberalism and populism culminating in incompatible political, social and economic models. All of this is intricately and certainly enmeshed in geopolitical space. If all this stands to reason, then here is a compelling argument to be made that the polycrisis as the norm will dictate what constitutes the new world order.

Towards a New World Order

The EU leadership, especially the French President Macron and the EU President Von der Leyden, is, in early 2023, very much focussed on a negotiated peace in the Russian-Ukraine war, trying to engage Chinese President Xi Jinping as a peace facilitator. However desirable this may be, there is one major problem, namely that Western politicians with some exceptions are still entrenched in a geopolitical status quo, namely USA unipolarity and its global hegemony, with a neoliberal ideology that governs the existing USA-led rules-based world order. This, however, is not acceptable to China. For example, by supporting Russia in the Ukraine-Russian war and circumventing the sanctions imposed by USA-led alliance of mostly European countries China is further detaching itself from the existing rules-based world order. This raises the question of potential 'new world order'. Prior to responding to this question, it may be useful to take a step back and provide a general contextual backdrop.

Within this context of 'new world orders' there are compelling arguments to be made that China is on its way to become an USA peer competitor and regional hegemon in large parts of the Global South, including Latin America, Africa and Asia. This applies inter alia to the provision of foreign aid through the China-led New Development Bank and other IFIs governed by, for example, the BRICS countries. Furthermore, since the beginning of the Ukraine-Russian war and the sanctions imposed by the NATO, EU and other countries, China is able to obtain Russian oil, gas and other commodities at advantageous prices. By forming an alliance with Russia, and other BRICS countries, China is forming a new coalition opposed to the existing USA hegemony. Thus, it is not in the interest of China to see a defeat of Russia in the Ukraine. In other words, if China supports Russia in the war against Ukraine, it simply weakens the USA's global hegemonic position and at the same time strengthens its own geopolitical hegemonic ambitions.

This re-balancing of global power structures is emerging due to the West's mistaken geopolitical world view. Since the dissolution of the USSR, with the USA as the global hegemon imposing its own interpretation of unipolar world order, the USA, and allies, presumed that China will become a member of the neoliberal world order and thus will support the Western international system, values, norms and institutions. However, since his ascendance to power in 2012, Xi Jinping has signalled that China is seeking a central position on the world stage corresponding to its military might and economic power, and a desire to restructure, change and re-define parts of the existing world order to better accommodate its own world views and interests. To do otherwise would be against its own geopolitical interests.

With this contextual background in mind, one may return to the question of a 'new' world order. The West adheres largely to a rules-based world order. This order consists of a series of rules and regulations which regulate the conduct of nations and international institutions. Dugard (2023: 223) summarises rules-based world order as being:

> Founded on a liberal international order... based on principles of democratic governance, the protection of individual rights, economic openness and the rule of law... characterized by equality, human rights, freedom, multilateralism, free movement of goods, and collective security. In content, it goes beyond the narrow positivist perception of international law to include soft law, including the standards and recommendations of international standard-setting organizations and conferences and rules made by non-state actors'

The rules are habitually codified through international agreements and treaties, and by institutions. As such they provide a framework for the conduct of international relations. In a rules-based world order, member states are required to follow the set rules and respect the authority of international institutions. Thus, member states are no longer anarchic entities because large parts of international relation powers are transferred to international institutions. The potential problem with the current situation whereby China and Russia are challenging the existing rules-based world order is the issue of polarities. Since the dissolution of the USSR the world was unipolar and the rules were set by the USA, as the global hegemon. However, with the rise of China as an economic and military power the world changed to a USA-Chinas bipolarity and if we consider Russia, and potentially other emerging powers, to multipolarity.

The problem of the current perception of a rules-based world order is that it is engulfed in a crisis. First, there is a crisis of rules legitimation, and second, there is the question of polarity. With reference to the latter, it should be sufficient to say that the USA-led Western alliance remains firmly grounded in the belief of a unipolar world, a belief strongly challenged by countries from the Global South. It is the rules-based concept of world order that contributes to a world in crises, depending on who sets the rules and what are the rules. In principle and practice the rules are set by the hegemonic power(s). Since WWII the rules were set by the USA and USSR, correspondingly, and for their own respective benefit. Since the end of the Cold War, the USA as the global hegemon set and interpreted the rules. Today, there is an alternative emerging.

From a political vantage point, the rules-based world order crisis in a context of the Russia-Ukraine war and other subsequently emerging crises, such as the food, humanitarian and development aid, economic and political crises, reveal broader challenges confronting world order. This calls for changing geopolitical realities and ensuring that international institutions, such as the UN, IMF, World Bank, WTO and others, are capable to respond to complex global challenges effectively and efficiently. In essence the contemporary crises concerning world order revolve around the competition between a value-based and a norms-based grounded 'new' world order, whereas the former represents the values of the hegemon, and the latter represents the norms set by consensus of the international community, such as the UN. As a consequence of the Russia-Ukraine war, the new world order is being determined by the USA-Ukraine-NATO axis, as much as by the PR China-Russia political and economic alignment. Given these two competing blocks the world is becoming increasingly a multilateral and a multipolar place, with multiple world orders. Thus, any norm-based world order(s) will have to give way to value-based world order(s).

If this stands to reason, and notwithstanding that Russia-Ukraine war will come to an end, one way or another, there is no guarantee that an economic war will suddenly end. The sanctions imposed on Russia by the Western alliance will continue to plague the world economies and by extension the developing world. The sanctions imposed by the Western alliance brought about inter alia economic, energy, food, migration and foreign aid crises.

The Economic War: Sanctions as Contributors to Polycrisis, and World Order(s)

Following the Russian invasion of Ukraine in 2022 the West sleep-walked into imposing a whole array of mostly economic sanction against Russia. The problem is that thus far sanctions did not work as envisaged by the Western allies. Russia has found new markets and trading partners at the detriment of the traditional European countries such as Germany. This is not surprising, for as history has shown sanctions are usually not successful. For example, the USA's sanctions imposed on Cuba some 50 years ago did not bring about a regime change. In 1979 the West imposed sanctions on Iran, but the Mullah regime is still in power. Western economic sanctions were imposed on Saddam Hussain's Iraq without much success. USA and some of its allies imposed sanctions on China, without many benefits, if any, for the USA. The current economic sanctions imposed on Russia by the USA-led Western coalition consisting of most EU and NATO countries have thus far turned out to be unsuccessful.

From the West's perspective the aim of the sanctions imposed on Russia is to weaken it and to bring it economically, politically and militarily to its knees. From the US-led Western alliance's vantage point, the sanctions would at least be an instrument to bring about a regime change and furthermore initiate a disintegration of the Russian Federation, not dissimilar to the break-up of the former USSR. This is simply not going to happen, for economically Russia is reorienting its economic focus towards East aligning itself with BRICS countries. Additionally, Russia is pursuing new economic alliances using soft power development aid in Africa, Asia and Latin America. At the same time, from a military perspective, it is important to remember that a disintegration of the Russian Federation would potentially be a world disaster. The vast arsenal of nuclear weapons that Russia possesses would be divided and would fall into the hands of some of the 21 Russian republics. Finally, if Western sanctions imposed on Russia were to be economically, political and militarily successful and Russia's government would feel an increased existential threat, it may consider its nuclear options.

In order to understand which sanctions may be effective, there is a need to take a step back and to find out what is Russia's Realpolitik in the case of Ukraine. That is, Putin must be aware that his initial aims of the special military operation in Ukraine are to a large extent illusionary. To put it differently, Putin has changed the Russian governments aims and objectives of the Ukraine invasion on numerous occasions, which may have been used to start to discuss issues concerning territorial integrity and claims. However, thus far NATO is in its current state of mind not capable, for it is almost single-mindedly focussed on winning the war against Russia. This brings us back to the thesis that Russia as the single largest nuclear power may use nuclear weapons if it feels that its existence is in danger. Setting aside NATO's current attitude, it leaves only the EU and China to take the lead in bringing the sanction war to an end and pursue a dialogue with Russia.

To be sure, the sanctions announced by the EU and the USA are severe. However, they are not supported by all states. Whether in Asia, Africa or Latin America, many states that have condemned Russia's war against Ukraine refuse to implement the sanctions. One can mention China, India or Malaysia, but also Mexico and the Persian Gulf states or Turkey, a NATO member. This weakens the effectiveness of sanctions, and their influence on the Russian economy is seriously diminished. In short, the sanctions have not 'torn to shreds' the Russian economy, as the former US President Obama suggested in 2014.

This brings back the question of sanctions as drivers of crises, which is hallmarked by a paradox. The Western sanctions imposed on Russia had a reverse effect. They brought about an energy crisis in the West, a food crisis in developing countries, a migration crisis in the EU, a foreign aid crisis by shifting aid money to military aid and the humanitarian crisis in the Ukraine. These are fuelled by at least four types of interrelated wars, namely, the military war fought as proxy war between the West (mainly NATO) and Russia, an economic war in the form of Western sanctions imposed on Russia, a propaganda war between the West and Russia and a geopolitical war.

Political Discontent: An Unholy Alliance between the Far Right and the Far Left

The existing polycrisis extends beyond the levels of politics pursued by governments, political and military blocks and international cum multilateral organisations. The polycrisis has reached as a trickle-down effect the general public on both sides of the political continuum. The impact of the Russia-Ukraine war is bringing about general public discontent with the governing parties' politics. For example, there were recently large demonstrations against the Russian-Ukraine war in Berlin, Prague and other European cities. In the Austrian parliament, the far right *Freiheitliche Partei* demonstrably left the Parliamentary Chamber in response to President Zelenskyy's address to the members of the lower house. Many of the parliamentary mostly left-wing of the centre left, Austrian Social Democrats (SPÖ), manifestly decided not to attend Zelenskyy's address. Setting aside discontent with the polycrisis at political rallies and actions a new phenomenon is emerging, namely a convergence of politics between the far right and the far left.

In the Global South, there is an increasing discontent with financial, military, diplomatic and economic support and attention which the USA-led Western allies are directing towards Ukraine. As covered in Chapter 4, much of the Global South and other countries outside Europe are affected by war and other crises. They experience economic hardship, and political turmoil, yet the crises in these countries receive only a portion of responsiveness shown to Ukraine. Subrahmanyam Jaishankar, Indian Foreign Minister, put it aptly when he said that the most affluent countries have treated Europe's problems as world problems, although the world problems are not perceived as Europe's problems. This discontent is a serious challenge for the USA-led Western alliance, engaged in a proxy war against Russia and addressing economic and political ambitions, and territorial claims and counterclaims, amidst an economic, military and political ascent of China's foreign aid.

Crises as a Continuum Revisited

As it stands, it is difficult to imagine that even with an end of the Russia-Ukraine war the main crises will disappear. According to the World Economic Forum (2023), the world's major existing cataclysms are energy, food, inflation and the overall cost of living crisis. Projecting into the future the, report identifies the cost-of-living crisis as the number one calamity and thus threat to global peace, followed by trade and technology crises. Others argue that the existing polycrisis will continue. Given the rise of geopolitical multipolarity the world will continue to have to confront the food, migration, economic, political, energy and supply chain crises. Each of these crises requires a separate discussion as well as a discussion about the interaction of the constituent crises, namely, the political, food, economic, energy, migration and supply chain crises. This is, of course, beyond the scope of this chapter. Thus, it shall suffice to highlight a few important factors contributing to the interregnum (Babic, 2020).

For example, the above-mentioned crises interact and exacerbate each other: (1) Food and Migration Crises: food insecurity can drive migration as people move in search of better living conditions and access to resources. This, in turn, can strain resources in the developed and developing countries, leading to further food shortages and potential military, political and go-political conflicts. (2) Economic and Political Crises: economic instability and inequality can fuel political unrest and lead to political and military crises. Conversely, political instability can undermine economic growth and exacerbate inequality, leading to further economic crises, engulfing developed and developing countries. (3) Energy and Supply Chain Crises: energy crises, such as fuel shortages or disruptions in electricity supply, can disrupt supply chains and lead to shortages of essential goods and services. Similarly, supply chain disruptions can lead to energy shortages and further disruptions to the economy. It is evident by now that a polycrisis can create complex and interconnected challenges that require multifaceted solutions which are currently absent, mainly due to the geo-political competitions.

Locating geopolitics within a context of foreign aid, as covered in Chapter 5, it is noteworthy that geopolitics, as an area of analysis, fell into disrepute after the Second World War but is now a vigorous and creative field, and has a great deal to tell us about the motivations for many current aid programmes. Geopolitics has, of course, been a crucial consideration in aid delivery for decades, and notably during the Cold War, and the current strategic competition between the USA and China is fuelling a new cold war with many similar results, with aid increasingly being used by both sides to buy, or leverage, support. It is also argued that geopolitical calculations have a fundamental influence on how the idea of development itself is conceptualised and operationalised – what is called the 'geopolitical imagination'. Given the growing influence of Chinese aid it is important to analyse its nature and particular characteristics, but there are sharp differences of opinion here. For some, China is attempting to gain privileged access to resources and is progressively luring governments into unsustainable levels of debt that can then be used to gain undue influence, the Chinese Debt Trap touched upon in Chapter 4. China is also propping up a number of undemocratic and authoritarian regimes, it is claimed. For others, China is providing a welcome challenge to the power of the traditional Western aid donors, allowing governments in the Global South to develop authentic and sustainable programmes of their own.

Ending the Russia-Ukraine War and the Rise of a 'New' World Order

As mentioned in preceding discussions, the Russia-Ukraine war and all other wars will end one way or another. But there is no geopolitical indication that the world will simply return to the USA-led rules-based world order. Given the rise of geopolitical multipolarity the world will need to get used to a different world order – perhaps a 'new' norms-based, rather than a values- or rules-based world order. This was already highlighted by Russia by using the Russia-Ukraine war as a conduit. In short, Russia declared its conditions, a new world order, as the West prepares the ground for peace talks. However, thus far there is no meaningful resolution to the Russo-Ukraine war on the horizon. The reason is that there is an incompatibility of the claims from the war parties.

As long as the war continues or even if a frozen conflict emerges, the unipolar world order cannot be maintained. Certainly, China will not join the USA-led western alliance. If anything, Russia will become politically and economically increasingly dependent on China, mostly as a junior partner, and PR China will heighten its position as a USA peer competitor. The China–Russia axis would undoubtedly try to change the existing USA-dominated world order, or more likely establish a new one in competition to latter. This would lead to a bipolar world order. However, the geopolitical situation is much more complex. There are political and economic blocks emerging in Africa, Latin America and the Middle East, which are non-aligned. It is not quite clear at the moment if any of these blocks will align themselves with a China-Russia alliance or form a non-aligned nations movement. Either way

the foreign policies and thus development aid agenda of the western international aid agencies will need to shift towards acceptance of a new world order.

Implications for Foreign Aid

The realities of foreign aid in this complex, contested space, riven with geopolitical tensions and great power competition, are potentially highly pessimis-
tic. Despite some highly contradictory outcomes in specific aid interventions,
some great progress has been made over the past few decades to address
poverty, and other indicators of human development and wellbeing, many of
which are contained within the SDGs, maternal mortality, health, education,
food security (until around 2015). Furthermore, aid is a very consistent, if
not sufficient, mechanism to address marginalisation and human development
objectives in spaces where the market cannot and likely will not provide opportunities required. The market fails in many ways, yet the greater the failures of neoliberalism, the more emphasis is put on neoliberal solutions within
a western liberal development paradigm. The new world order(s) debated at
a very high level across this volume will be the context in which political
economic ideology will evolve. The greatest danger in all of this is the potential for foreign aid, global development and even humanitarian relief to be
further politicised and weaponised in pursuit of geostrategic objectives. That
aid is used in this way, as shown in this volume, is neither new nor surprising. Yet, the geostrategic impact of aid appears to be increasing in importance
with regard to decisions made as to the modality, conditions and target of aid.
Decades of discourse in seeking alternatives to western-led neoliberal globalised foreign aid contexts are ignored, in the pursuit of a liberal rules-based
western-led world order.

In international affairs we are now witnessing a geopolitical contest of epic
proportions. This involves attempts to gain support from all nations, however
small, and an increasingly bitter contest to control markets as well as access to
resources. Foreign aid programmes have become an integral part of this global
contest – indeed from the high-level analysis in this volume, it is not a stretch
to consider that aid has now become weaponised. The geostrategic drivers
of aid targeting and modalities are clear. In Africa, as we have demonstrated,
aid is integral to this competition, and in the South Pacific – previously seen
as a rather sleepy regions rather isolated from major global events – small
island nations are now on the geopolitical frontline. Competition in this new
Cold War – mirroring the experience of Soviet Period – allows some countries to play off the two sides, but research has shown that aid programmes
implemented for essentially political reasons are generally less effective than
properly thought-out development strategies.

Given the many complex challenges to this vision of the future, it is critical
to consider the potential impact and drivers of foreign aid. In a context where
one of the key impacts of a polycrisis is the reversal of decades of progress in

human development, it is difficult to see where foreign aid may be best lever-aged to reverse the decline in global development and address the complexi-ties of climate change, economic instability and debt crises, food insecurity, vast and undealt with inequalities, forced migration and many other issues that are felt much more keenly by those outside the categorisation of 'rich' and getting richer. In essence aid can be a useful contribution to the international development effort, but the weaponisation of aid will have detrimental effects, and there is an absolute imperative to consider the geopolitical and geostrate-gic drivers of aid, explicitly.

Conclusion

Considering the ways in which the polycrisis has developed, it is essential to consider how the major crises of the 21st century – the Global Financial Cri-sis, the Covid pandemic, the competition between the USA and China and the war in Ukraine, in particular – have built on each other and interacted in com-plex, compounding and novel ways. This has represented a major challenge to the old international order: we might even say that this liberal international or-der has been dealt a fatal blow. The ways in which these dramatic events have had a major impact on the aims and implementation of international develop-ment and the provision of foreign aid are also considered. A key issue now is how the global economy will change in response to this polycrisis as well as ongoing technological change, and the implications for the Global South. It appears that the dominant neoliberal paradigm is in retreat, and globalisation is in retreat in the face of growing economic nationalism, with massive sub-sidies being used to reverse the 'offshoring' of recent years. Multilateralism among some of the core international places of the liberal economic order is challenged form within and without. Great power conflicts will continue, and the implications for those most marginalised are showing clearly and un-equivocally to be critical, and unaddressed in many ways that matter. We may well be seeing the emergence of a new global international order, and it may be much more challenging for the Global South than the older one. Yet the polycrisis context demonstrates clearly that nobody is immune to the complex impacts of the crisis of modernity that we face. To use power, influence and relatedly foreign aid, in any way other than to promote some liveable, surviv-able future for all is indeed an anathema.

References

Babic, M. (2020). Let's talk about the interregnum: Gramsci and the crisis of the liberal world order. *International Affairs, 96*(3), 767–786. https://doi.org/10.1093/ia/iiz254

Dugard, J. (2023). The choice before us: International law or a 'rules-based interna-tional order'? *Leiden Journal of International Law, 36*(2), 223–232. https://doi.org/10.1017/S0922156523000043

Transparency International (2022). Corruption Perception Index 2021. https://www.
    transparency.org/en/cpi/2021?gclid=CjwKCAjwue6hBhBVEiwA9YTx8P6rPfHgz-
    7F6rdHJEAWSFbw_tSA_TozLwiTQpcK66jP4MPrzca5cBoCbdoQAvD_BwE
World Economic Forum (2023). *The Global Risk Report* (18th ed.): Insight Report.
    Cologny/Geneva: World Economic Forum.

Index